OTHER BOOKS BY NATHANIEL BRANDEN

Taking Responsibility
The Six Pillars of Self-Esteem
The Art of Self-Discovery
The Power of Self-Esteem
Judgment Day: My Years with Ayn Rand
How to Raise Your Self-Esteem
To See What I See and Know What I Know
Honoring the Self
If You Could Hear What I Cannot Say
What Love Asks of Us (with Devers Branden)
The Psychology of Romantic Love
The Disowned Self
Breaking Free
The Psychology of Self-Esteem
Who Is Ayn Rand?

NATHANIEL BRANDEN

THE
ART OF
LIVING
CONSCIOUSLY

The Power of Awareness to Transform Everyday Life

A Fireside Book
Published by Simon & Schuster

FIRESIDE
Rockefeller Center
1230 Avenue of the Americas
New York, NY 10020

First Fireside Edition 1999

FIRESIDE and colophon are
registered trademarks of Simon & Schuster Inc.

Designed by Elina D. Nudelman

Manufactured in the United States of America

10 9 8 7

The Library of Congress has cataloged the
Simon & Schuster edition as follows:

Branden, Nathaniel.
    The art of living consciously: the power of
awareness to transform everyday life / Nathaniel
Branden.
        p. cm.
    Includes bibliographical references and index.
    1. Awareness.   2. Self-perception.   3. Conduct
of life.   I. Title.
BF311.B715   1997
158.1—dc21   96-49721   CIP
ISBN-13: 978-0-684-81084-3
ISBN-10:   0-684-81084-0
ISBN-13: 978-0-684-83849-6 (Pbk)
ISBN-10:   0-684-83849-4 (Pbk)

CONTENTS

CONTENTS

This earth is the distant star we must find a way to reach.

Introduction

A few months after completing my previous book, *Taking Responsibility,* I was at a dinner party, and someone asked me what I was writing next. I answered that I was about to embark on a book that would examine what it means to live consciously.

An older woman, her face lined with bitterness, frowned and shook her head disapprovingly. "Live consciously?" she said. "Not a good idea. Who would want to live consciously? Life would be too painful."

I asked, "Is it less painful if we live unconsciously and mechanically, without knowing what we are doing, and blind to opportunities to make things better?" But she did not answer.

Someone else at the table remarked, "Well, even if living consciously does have advantages—isn't it still a lot of *work?*"

▲ ▲ ▲

**Like a light that can be turned brighter or
dimmer, consciousness exists on a continuum.**

▼

It is true that living consciously obliges us at times to confront painful realities. It is also true that it demands an effort. As a way of operating in the world, living consciously has its costs, and we will examine them. A central theme of this book, however, is that the rewards are overwhelmingly greater than any apparent drawback. Living consciously is a source of power and liberation. It does not weigh us down—it lifts us up.

Like a light that can be turned brighter or dimmer, consciousness exists on a continuum. We can be more conscious or less conscious, more aware or less aware. So the choice is not between absolute optimal consciousness and literal unconsciousness (as in a coma). The choice is between living more consciously and less consciously. Or we might say: between living consciously and living mechanically. And it is always a matter of degree.

The tragedy of so many people is precisely that, to a great extent, they live mechanically: their thinking is stale, they don't examine their motives, and they respond to events automatically. They rarely take a fresh look at anything and rarely have a new thought. They exist at a low or shallow level of awareness. One of the consequences is that they live lives drained of color, excitement, or passion. It is not difficult to see that consciousness energizes, while its absence produces boredom and enervation.

To live consciously is to be committed to awareness as a way of being in the world and to bring to each activity a level of awareness appropriate to it. But what this means is not obvious. "Living consciously" is an enormous abstraction. We will examine its meaning in the chapters that follow.

I use *consciousness* here in its primary meaning: the state of being conscious or aware of some aspect of reality. Why is consciousness important? The short answer is that for all species that possess it, consciousness is the basic tool of survival and of adaptation to reality—the ability to be aware of the environment in some way, at some level, and to guide action accordingly. One might as well ask: Why is sight important?

Living consciously is a state of being mentally active rather than passive. It is the ability to look at the world through fresh eyes. It is intelligence taking joy in its own function. Living consciously is seeking to be aware of everything that bears on our interests, actions, values, purposes, and goals. It is the willingness to confront facts, pleasant or unpleasant. It is the desire to discover our mistakes and correct them. Within the range of our interests and concerns, it is the quest to keep expanding our awareness and understanding, both of the world external to self and of the world within. It is respect for reality and respect for the distinction between the real and the unreal. It is the commitment to see what we see and know what we know. It is recognition that the act of dismissing reality is the root of all evil.

▲ ▼ ▲

The issue of living consciously versus unconsciously takes many forms. Here are two examples taken from my practice of psychotherapy, in which we can see what living *un*consciously may look like. Note that these examples merely illustrate the problem; they do not yet suggest the path to a solution.

Arnold K. was a forty-seven-year-old professor of history who imagined he was deeply in love with his wife and was unkind to her in a hundred ways he did not notice. When she needed to talk to him about something of importance to her, he typically was preoccupied, only half listened, and rarely responded in any meaningful way. When she expressed a desire, he smiled and said nothing and soon drifted off to another subject. When she disagreed with him, he swung off into another monologue without dealing with what she had said. When she tried to tell him of ways he hurt her, he did not hear, or apologized instantly and forgot her words within an hour. He knew how devoted he felt, so he believed he was a loving husband. And when the mood struck, he could be truly generous, considerate, and caring. Essentially, however, he lived in a private cocoon that contained himself and his love for her and his image of her but not the actual woman: she was exiled to that foreign realm, reality. So that in real-world terms, she was not part of his marriage. His wife was not the woman he lived with; he lived with a fantasy existing only inside his head. In some subjective sense of his own he may have loved her, but he did not love her *consciously,* did not day by day give the relationship the awareness it needed and deserved. Eventually she became ill and abruptly was gone from his life. Standing at her graveside in agony, he saw that during the twelve years of their marriage he had not been there—he had been lost inside his own mind. He saw that he had abandoned his wife long before she had "abandoned" him (by dying). What love had not accomplished, death had accomplished: jolted him into waking up, at least for a time.

For many of us, suffering is the only teacher to whom we listen. In Arnold's case, as with the case below, suffering precipitated the decision to seek psychotherapy.

Rebecca L. was a thirty-nine-year-old leader of personal growth workshops. She saw herself as a person who was on a spiritual path and who had attained a high level of consciousness, yet she was oblivious to the wreckage she had created in her family life. Her lofty view of herself was based on the fact that she was a student of the *I Ching,* took classes in Tantric Yoga, immersed herself in the literature of the contemplative traditions, and had had thirteen years of Jungian analysis. She subjected her two teenage daughters to endless hours of psychological interpretation of their behavior. At dinner she would invite her husband to tell his dreams, which she would then proceed to analyze. If any of her interpretations were challenged, she would respond with gentle compassion; if the challenge persisted, she became first irritated and then increasingly angry—until everyone retreated into sullen exhaustion. She could quote interminably from many spiritual masters and had no idea that in the privacy of their bedroom her daughters would sometimes talk about how pleasant life could be if only mother would die. Her husband did not appear to indulge in daydreams; he merely barricaded himself behind his work and spent as little time alone with her as possible. She moved through her life in a kind of trance while priding herself on being more "awake," more "conscious," than those around her. She could not understand why she so often felt a vague, generalized anxiety.

Neither of these people was asleep in the literal sense, and neither was awake in the sense required for a successful life. Their stories give us a preliminary sense of the territory we need to explore—or, more precisely, certain aspects of it; we will see that there are many others.

▲ ▼ ▲

Sometimes, when we reflect on our life and on the mistakes we have made and regretted, it seems to us we were sleeping when we imagined we were awake. We wonder how we could have failed to see that which now stands out in such bold relief. Of course, this may be self-deceiving, in that hindsight always sees more clearly. At that earlier time, we may have been as conscious as we knew how to be.

However, sometimes our sense of having been sleepwalking through our existence reflects an accurate assessment. We know we were not mindful when we needed to be. Our awareness was diffuse or distracted rather than focused and disciplined. No doubt there were reasons, but reasons do not alter facts. In retrospect, we wish we had been more conscious.

We think, for example, of all the danger signals we had ignored at the start of what turned out to be a disastrous love affair—for example, our lover's incongruous behavior, conflicting statements, mysterious nonexplanations, sudden and inexplicable emotional outbursts. We ask ourselves, Where was my mind at the time? Or we remember all the warnings our supervisor gave us long before we were discharged, and we wonder why the words did not penetrate. Or we reflect on the opportunities we let slip by because in our trancelike state we did not appreciate them for what they were, and we ask ourselves how that was possible. Where was I, we wonder, when my life was happening?

When I discussed the practice of living consciously in previous books, it was exclusively from the perspective of its importance to self-esteem. Here, the focus is wider. What does it mean to act consciously? To love consciously? To parent consciously? To feel consciously? To work consciously? To struggle consciously? To vote consciously? To legislate consciously? To address the great issues of life consciously?

To offer an example from the political realm: When legislators pass laws on the expediency of the moment, such as price and wage controls, without thinking through the long-term, foreseeable consequences of their programs, which unfortunately is the pattern of most legislation—and the results are worse than the problem the legislation promised to correct, which is so often the case—an entire nation pays the price for that lack of appropriate consciousness (and conscientiousness).[1]

Almost all of us tend to operate more consciously in some areas than in others. We may bring great consciousness to our work and very little to our personal relationships—or vice versa. We may think far more clearly about our careers than about our political beliefs—or vice versa. We may maintain a high level of mental focus in matters pertaining to our health and a low level in matters pertaining to ethics or religion—or vice versa.

In this book, I examine what operating consciously means across the broad spectrum of human concerns—from dealing with our most intimate emotions, to pursuing a career, to falling in love, to sustaining a marriage, to rearing children, to meeting the challenges of the workplace, to choosing the values that guide our actions, to understanding what self-esteem depends on, to weighing the claims offered by religion and mysticism.

With regard to this last, for many years my readers have been asking me how my concept of living consciously relates to issues of spirituality, religion, mysticism, and the ethical teachings associated with mysticism, and I am happy to have an opportunity to answer them in print. For those with this particular interest, chapters 1 and 7 may be read as a self-contained unit.

▲ ▼ ▲

Our need to live consciously, with the meaning I develop in this book, is intrinsic to the human condition. But it has acquired a new urgency in the modern age. The more rapid the rate of change, the more dangerous it is to live mechanically, relying on routines of belief and behavior that may be irrelevant or obsolete.

Further, old structures and old traditions are falling away. The voices of official authority grow ever fainter and command less and less respect. Our culture seems to have dissolved or exploded into ten thousand mutually adversarial subcultures. Even committed conformists are finding it increasingly difficult to know what to conform to, so splintered and fragmented has our world become. We are obliged to *choose* the values by which we live. We are obliged to *choose* more and more aspects of our existence— from where we reside to what career we pursue to what lifestyle we select to what religion or philosophy we embrace. In earlier periods of our history, we were born into societies where all these choices were, figuratively, made for us by custom and tradition— that is, by people who lived before us. But that time is gone and will not come again. Today we are exposed to an unprecedented amount of information and an unprecedented number of options. We are thrown on our own resources as never before. And we have nothing to protect us but the clarity of our thinking.

The fact that we have evolved from an agricultural economy to a manufacturing economy to an information economy has its own powerful implications for the value of living consciously. The age of the muscle-worker is past; this is the age of the mind-worker. That our mind is our basic tool of survival is not new; what is new is that this fact has become inescapably clear. The market is rapidly diminishing for people who have nothing to contribute but physical labor. In an economy in which knowledge, information, creativity—and their translation into innovation—are the prime source of wealth, what is needed above all is *minds*. What is needed are people who are willing and able *to think*.

▲ ▲ ▲

If we wish to remain adaptive, we must be committed to *continuous learning* as a way of life.

▼

And since knowledge is growing at a rate unprecedented in human history, and the training we received yesterday is inadequate to the requirements of tomorrow, if we wish to remain adaptive, we must be committed to *continuous learning* as a way of life. Today, this is one of the meanings of living consciously.

Whether our focus is on preserving and strengthening family ties in a world of increasingly unstable human relationships, or on gaining access to a decent job, or on growing and evolving as a person, or on guiding a company through the stormy seas of a fiercely competitive global marketplace—whether our goals are material, emotional, or spiritual—the price of success is the same: consciousness; thinking; learning. To be asleep at the wheel—to rely only on the known, familiar, and automatized—is to invite disaster.

We have entered the mind millennium. This book is a wake-up call.

1

Living Consciously: First Principles

● LIVING consciously has its roots in respect for reality—a respect for facts and truth. In this chapter, we will explore what this means.

Let me say at the outset that no one is born with this reality orientation. It must be learned. Its full realization represents an achievement—and unfortunately, roadblocks are often thrown in a child's way. Instead of supporting a child's natural impulse to grow in awareness and cognitive maturity, adults acting out their own problems may behave in ways that tempt a child not to open his or her eyes wider but to shut them.

Being a child can be very difficult. One commonly witnesses adult behavior that is frightening, bewildering, inexplicable. One cannot make sense of it. Confidence in one's mind may be subverted. One's sense of reality may be undercut. Consciousness may be experienced as futile or even dangerous.

Mother, for example, gives a solemn talk on the importance of honesty. Then guests arrive, and Mother makes statements to them the child knows to be untrue. The child searches Mother's face for a hint that might dissolve this mystery. Mother looks back at him, her face guileless and guiltless, and not a word of explanation is offered, then or later. The hypocrisy—the contradiction—is a fact treated as a nonfact.

Or a child sits at the dinner table with her mother and two brothers, and Mother is talking to them pleasantly and does not turn her head when Father staggers toward them, reeking of alcohol and stumbling as he advances. Father pulls out a chair, misses it, and hits the floor instead, where he remains, half-lying, half-sitting. And Mother goes on talking as if nothing had happened, which is her characteristic response whenever anything unpleasant takes place. The child's eyes swing from Father to Mother to the two brothers and then back to Father again. But no acknowledgment of Father's state is made by anyone. The message is clear: a fact that one denies (evades) is not a fact.

Or a child cannot understand why Teacher so often ridicules her over the smallest mistakes or speaks to her in a voice heavy with sarcasm—this same teacher who speaks so often about the importance of addressing everyone with courtesy and respect. "Don't you like me?" the child gathers the courage to ask, and the teacher replies, her eyes glittering with irritation, "I love all my students." The child does not dare to push further by saying, "Then why do you make us all afraid of you?" The child knows this is a question that will never be answered; she will merely be offered another lie and perhaps another sarcastic reproach. Truth is expendable in a game whose rules are never stated.

Inside the minds of children such as these a deeper question struggles inarticulately but is never asked: *How am I to live in your world?*

And inside that question are other questions: How am I to know what to believe if you don't mean what you say or say what you mean? How can I trust if I never know when I am being lied to? How can I feel safe if facts are not treated as facts? And with you as my guide, how I am even to understand? How am I to know what *anything* is? And if I can't know—how am I to live?

▲ ▲ ▲

**Children need love, true enough, but they also
need the experience of living in a rational
universe.**

▼

The danger to a child confronted with human irrationality is
that he or she will surrender *the will to understand*—the will to
make sense out of experience. The child may give up the belief
that thinking is worthwhile.

Children need love, true enough, but they also need the experience of living in a rational universe. And it is just this experience
that too many parents fail to provide.

By a "rational universe," I mean an environment in which facts
are treated as facts, truth is respected, question-asking is valued,
not punished, and people do not permit themselves contradictions
and do not assail others with conflicting messages. I mean an
environment in which adults speak to a child's *mind,* not to his or
her *fears*—and in which a child's desire to understand is honored
and nurtured.

▲ ▲ ▲

**Living consciously is a challenge for all of us
—even when there is no trauma to overcome.**

▼

Sometimes the assaults on a child's will to understand are nothing more than the familiar adult irrationalities of everyday life:
the broken promises, the contradictory injunctions, the denial of
obvious truths. Sometimes, however, the assaults are more dramatic. I remember an incident many years ago when I was treating
a woman who had been sexually molested by her father when
she was five years old. Under hypnosis she partially relived the
experience; I wanted to learn the silent thoughts that had accom-
panied the episode. What impressed me most was the focus of the

trauma. It was not on the pain or even the sense of violation, per se. *It was the inability to comprehend how her father could be doing such a thing.* "He's my *daddy,*" she kept saying. "How can he be doing this?" Later, out of hypnosis, she remarked, "That was the worst horror—that the experience totally blew up any notion I had of reason or sanity. What Daddy was doing was impossible. Yet he was doing it." The trauma was compounded when she tried to tell her mother what had happened; her mother kept moving about the kitchen, doing small chores and muttering pleasantly some variant of "Your father and I love you" and "No need to make yourself unhappy." Her father's demeanor reflected not a trace of what had taken place between them. The crime against the child's body was less than the crime against her mind. In therapy, it was easier to awaken my client's interest in new relationships than to awaken her interest in living consciously: she had spent too many years surviving by keeping the light of awareness turned down to a tolerable level of dimness. To turn that light up was a challenge.

However, we will see that even when there is no trauma to overcome, to live consciously is a challenge for all of us.

ACQUIRING A SENSE OF REALITY

To live consciously, we need to develop what I call "a sense of reality." What does this idea entail?

Right now, you are holding a book in your hands. You are secure in the knowledge that the book will not suddenly turn into a telephone or a cup of coffee. If you close the book and go for a walk, you are secure in the knowledge that your home will not turn into an automobile in your absence. You know that change is possible to the book or your home, of course—for example, if your dog chews the book up or if a hurricane hits your home—but you are secure in the knowledge that those changes will be lawful, in accordance with the nature of the materials of which the book and your home are made. The book may be chewed up, but it will not turn into ice cream. Your house may be destroyed, but it will not be transformed into a bicycle. If we are able to move through reality with some measure of assurance, the ultimate (metaphysical) root of our certainty is the knowledge that *things are what they are*. In philosophy, this principle is known as the law of identity. A is A. A thing is itself. This is at once the ultimate statement about existence and the first law of logic.

The law of identity gives birth to the law of causality: a thing must act in accordance with its nature. In any given set of circumstances, what it will *do* is determined—caused—by what it *is*.[1]

Although the above examples do involve physical entities, a "thing" need not be a physical object. A "thing" used here as an equivalent to an "existent" can be an entity, an attribute, an action, a thought, an intention, an inner emotional state, a form of energy —whatever *is*.

Ultimately, any security we feel in this world, any sense of living in a stable universe, is traceable to the axiom of identity. It is so intrinsic to all our experience that we never think about it explicitly, unless we are philosophers. But it is the foundation of everything. What is, is; what is not, is not. Nothing is more certain, and nothing is more fundamental.

This said, let us reflect briefly on two concepts that underlie all our others and are the most basic of all: existence and nonexistence.

Or, in simpler language: something and nothing.

▲ ▲ ▲

To be, is to be *something*.

▼

The concept of *something* applies to every concept in your mind, to the entire content of your consciousness, and to the total of your knowledge, regardless of the amount or degree of your knowledge. It is *the* fundamental concept of consciousness—it marks the start of being conscious. When a baby opens its eyes and receives its first sensations of sight or sound, all that its consciousness can register is awareness of *something*. The baby does not know *what* it is and does not yet possess any concepts, but we who are adults know that the concept of *something* names the first state and stage of the baby's awareness. The blob of light he senses is *something*. The sound she hears is *something*. The blanket he touches is *something*. To be conscious is to be conscious of something.

In the development of a baby's consciousness, the next step after the grasping of *something* is the ability to perceive *entities*. This is made possible by the ability of the brain and nervous system to retain and integrate disparate sensations.[2] It is with this ability that knowledge proper begins.

That which does not exist is *nothing*. We often use the concept of nothing to convey the absence of specific things. We say, "I have nothing in my pocket," meaning there are no physical objects in my pocket. Or we say, "The amount of my fortune is zero," meaning I have no money. But the metaphysical meaning of nothing is *nonexistence*. The literal void. The blank. The zero. Nonexistence does not exist. *Nothing* is a concept pertaining exclusively to a relation: it has meaning only in relation to *something* and denotes its absence. Nothing by itself is—nothing. It is not just another kind of something.

One expression of "a sense of reality" is the ability to grasp this simple fact. There is a tendency in mystical literature to treat "nothing" (or "emptiness") as a superior kind of "something."

To be something means to be something specific, as distinguished from the blank of nothing. To be something specific means to be an existent of a certain kind, a certain nature, a certain *identity*. The *identity* of a thing is that which it *is*.

And that which it is, *it is*. A rock is a rock. An electron is an electron. A fleeting feeling is a fleeting feeling. An unachieved ambition is an unachieved ambition. This inescapable truth is the basis of the laws of logic and of all rational thought. Defy it and thought has no coherence. Attempt to argue against it and one will still find oneself counting on it, as in the premise that one's claim is one's claim and not the opposite.

Not to possess an identity, not to possess a nature, not to be anything in particular, means not to be *anything,* which means not to exist. To be, is to be something.

▲ ▼ ▲

In the field of logic, the law of identity has a corollary, a companion principle it immediately entails. The law of noncontradiction states that nothing can be A and not-A at the same time and in the same respect. Nothing can be an attribute and not an attribute, true and not true, a fact and not a fact, *at the same time and in the same respect.* A rug cannot be white and not white, a proposition cannot be true and false, an event cannot be happening and not happening, at the same time and in the same respect. If we know anything, we know this. It is intrinsic to the act of being conscious—that is, aware of reality.[3]

To arrive at a contradiction is to know that we have made an error in our thinking. An example of a contradiction would be the claim that one has seen two mountains side by side without a valley between them. Or that one is a thoroughly honest politician who lies only when it is necessary to be elected. Or that one is absolutely certain that no one can know anything with certainty. Irrationalists (of whom there are many today) may wish to maintain a contradiction and call it "a higher level of knowledge." But the truth is, they have undercut that which makes knowledge possible. To persist in contradiction is to short-circuit consciousness itself. But then what is left in its stead? This issue is examined further in chapter 7, "Consciousness and Spirituality."

What confuses some people about this issue and allows them to imagine that contradictions are possible is that they do not pay sufficient attention to the qualifier "at the same time and in the same respect." Aristotle, the father of logic, was very precise in these matters. People say, for example, "Mr. B. is self-responsible at work but very irresponsible in his personal life. So he is and is not self-responsible. Therefore, contradictions are possible." The error here is that this is not a contradiction—not if one factors in time and respect. With greater precision, we say, "Mr. B. is self-responsible in some contexts but not in others. He is self-responsible some of the time, when he is operating his business, and irresponsible at other times, in the conduct of his personal life."

Sometimes we believe two statements are contradictory and later discover they are not, by expanding our knowledge to include a frame of reference in which a seeming incompatibility dissolves. For example, a person with only a limited understanding of the terms "religious" and "spiritual" might assume it is contradictory to say, "He is not religious, although he is very spiritual." A deeper understanding, however, would disclose that the presumed contradiction is only illusory.

Consider what contradictions mean in action. For example, consider the impact on a child's mind who receives the following parental messages: (1) We want you to be independent and learn to think for yourself; (2) We want you to obey our instructions and never question our judgment; (3) You are never to raise or discuss the discrepancy between the first injunction and the second. Students of development observe that this is one of the ways one destroys a consciousness before it is fully matured. And for this reason, it is difficult to think kindly of a parent who might respond, "I contradict myself? Very well, I contradict myself."

▲ ▲ ▲

Most people are unaware that their thinking and value system may be riddled with contradictions.

▼

Here are other instances of teachings that do violence to a young mind as A and not-A fight to occupy the same space: "Ours is a god of love and infinite benevolence, and if you do not embrace him, he will make you burn forever in hell." "Don't ask questions, don't try to understand—be reasonable." "It is a virtue to be thrifty, industrious, and hardworking, but if you commit the sin of succeeding, remember that it will be easier for a camel to pass through the eye of a needle than for a rich man to enter the kingdom of heaven." "Sex is dirty, rotten, and disgusting, and you should save it for your husband."

Most people, of course, do not embrace contradictions righteously. They are unaware they have them, unaware their thinking and value system may be riddled with them. That is why they are so often morally confused as to the proper course of action.

One of the most common forms in which people confront contradictions in everyday life is when their official view of themselves (their self-concept) clashes with some aspect of their behavior. In such a situation, they have three alternatives:

They can revise their self-concept.

They can change their behavior.

Or they can evade the contradiction.

The third option seems the most popular, perhaps because options one and two can be difficult. In such cases, the motive is to protect the evaders' self-esteem, or their pretense at it. But in fact they undermine self-esteem, because at a deeper level *they know what they are doing.* Evasion may deceive the conscious mind; it does not deceive the subconscious mind. Somewhere there is the knowledge: I am at odds with reality; I hold myself together by avoidance and denial.[4]

To offer an example from the wider, social sphere, we can observe that governments are notorious for pursuing contradictory policies. Example: waging a campaign against smoking while providing agricultural subsidies for tobacco growers. Indeed, it would be a major step toward cleaning up our legislative and regulatory mess if it were made a matter of law that contradictory policies could not be tolerated: one or the other (or both) had to be re-

scinded. In every domain, the law of noncontradiction is an effective broom for sweeping up refuse.

▲ ▲ ▲

**We undermine our self-esteem when we
persist in our contradictions, because at a
deeper level *we know what we are doing.***

▼

The laws of identity and noncontradiction are more than principles of logic: they are protectors of our sanity. Ignore them and we
eject ourselves from reality.

More than a few philosophers have broken themselves against
these laws when attempting to argue that such principles are not
immutable facts but mere conventions or no more than merely
probable. They inevitably expose themselves to the rebuttal that
they are presupposing that which they wish to attack: they are
obliged to count on these principles, use them, implicitly accept
their truth in any attempt to defeat them. No amount of intellectual squirming can efface the fact that when one makes any assertion, one implies that one's assertion is what it is and not the
opposite—and that if one's position is true, it is not simultaneously
and in the same respect false. The laws of identity and noncontradiction cannot be escaped.

Further, with regard to the *objectivity* of truth, if A is A, if facts
are facts, then things are what they are regardless of our agreement, knowledge, or belief. If something is a fact, our ignorance
of it or our refusal to see it does not render it a nonfact. That
which exists is what it is, independent of anyone's knowledge,
judgment, beliefs, hopes, wishes, or fears. (And this applies fully
as much to internal facts as to external ones: If I am feeling
something—say, fear, hurt, anger, envy, lust—I am feeling it,
whether or not I admit it.) Reality is that which exists, and the
function of consciousness is to perceive it. Reality is the *object* of
consciousness—the object that consciousness perceives and must
learn to perceive correctly.[5]

Thus, if I am an embezzler, I am an embezzler—that is reality —whether or not my crime is ever discovered. If I have appropriated the achievements of another and claimed them as my own, then I am a fraud—that is a fact—no matter how much the world acclaims me. If my partner becomes addicted to drugs, then that is her condition—that's the way things are—whether or not I ever admit it to myself. If I dislike being a parent, that is the truth of my feelings—that is reality—no matter how passionately I tell myself otherwise. If a new discovery contradicts and disconfirms my beliefs in some area, that is a fact—that is what is so—regardless of whether or not I choose to think about it.

If I live consciously, I do not attempt to evade facts: I do not imagine that blindness annihilates existence.

▲ ▲ ▲

In aligning ourselves with reality as best we understand it, we optimize our chances for success.

▼

Living consciously reflects the understanding that since we live in reality and must adapt to it if we are to survive and flourish, our first responsibility is to see clearly that which bears on our existence and well-being—more specifically, on our actions, interests, needs, values, and goals. The purpose of such sight is to guide behavior accordingly.

Living consciously reflects the recognition that, in aligning ourselves with reality as best we understand it, we optimize our chances for success—and that in setting ourselves against reality, we condemn ourselves to failure and possibly destruction. With respect to this second policy, consider the person who refuses to confront the unsolved problems in his marriage—on the implicit premise that if we don't talk about them, they won't exist—whose partner finally gives up in despair and leaves; or the person who dies from a disease because she refused to admit the reality of the disease and the need for treatment, on the often explicit premise that all sickness is an illusion and that so long as I don't believe I'm sick, I'll remain healthy. (That our beliefs can sometimes affect the course of an illness is an entirely different matter that in no way contradicts the point being made here.)

Living consciously reflects the conviction that sight is preferable to blindness; that respect for the facts of reality yields more satisfying results than defiance of the facts of reality; that evasion does not make the unreal real or the real unreal; that I am better served by correcting my mistakes than by pretending they do not exist; and that the more conscious I am of facts bearing on my life and goals, the more wisely and effectively I can act.

All of these interwoven realizations are what I mean by a sense of reality. They are the rock on which a conscious life stands.

AWARENESS: OUTER AND INNER

▲ ▲ ▲

Our inner world, too, is part of reality.

▼

When we begin to reflect on what it means to live consciously, we may find ourselves thinking in terms of paying attention to our environment, seeking to understand the world around us, looking for evidence that tells us if we are right or mistaken in our assumptions, searching out information that bears on our goals, learning more about our work, and other matters pertaining to the world external to self. That is all correct, but it is only half the story. The other half of living consciously has to do with self-awareness— with a concern to understand the inner world of needs, motives, thoughts, mental states, emotions, and bodily feelings.

If the essence of rationality is respect for the facts of reality, that must include the facts of one's own being. Our inner world, too, is part of reality. Mind is as real as matter. No one can be said to be living consciously who exempts self-awareness and self-examination from the agenda.

We all know people who are full of information about the external world and may be very observant in certain situations but who are utterly oblivious to their inner processes and the meaning of those processes. These people exist in an acute state of alien- ation. They have no interest concerning their own inner world— the world of needs, emotions—which often makes them ineffective in the external (social) world.

If we are to function effectively, we must learn to look in two directions—to preserve contact with the world and with the self. For example, if we are to achieve some particular goal, we need to know the objective requirements of a given situation *and* its emotional meaning to us. We need to know the facts *and* our appraisal of the facts. We need to know what we must do *and* what we feel about what we must do. In the literal moment of action, we may not choose to focus on our feelings (or we may, depending on circumstances), but as a rule, it is dangerous to be oblivious to the personal significance of situations. Such information can help us navigate appropriately.

▲ ▲ ▲

**If we are to function effectively, we must learn
to look in two directions: to preserve contact
with the world and with the self.**

▼

When a person decides, as a basic pattern of behavior, to disregard external reality when it suits him or her and surrender to the control of feelings, the chief feeling left to experience is anxiety. If we choose to move through life blindly, we have good reason to be afraid. To some extent this was the problem of Rebecca L., whose self-absorption made her oblivious to the effect of her behavior on her family or the hostility she engendered. Her anxiety was her organism's alarm signal, warning her of danger.

When a person decides, as a general policy, to cut off contact with emotions in order to function effectively in external reality, he or she sabotages the ability to think in key areas. If we disconnect from our personal context, we cannot then operate rationally in the personal realm: we have lost the knowledge of what things mean to us.

▲▲▲

**If we choose to move through life blindly, we
have good reason to be afraid.**

▼

What we are blind to in the world tends to reflect what we are blind to in ourselves. A person who denies the presence of a need tends to be blind to opportunities to satisfy that need—as, for instance, when a person denies his need and desire for companionship, suffers loneliness, and does not see opportunities for friendship. A person who denies the reality of her pain tends to be oblivious to the source of the pain and continually exposes herself to new hurt—as when a woman repeatedly subjects herself to exploitative and enervating encounters with men. A person who guiltily disowns certain of his desires may, via the mechanism of projection, attribute them to others—as when we refuse to recognize our feelings of envy while falsely attributing them to others.

The point is, awareness must flow freely in both directions or it will flow freely in neither. We will look at this issue in more detail in our discussion of reason and emotion. However, I want to relate two stories here that will add some preliminary clarification concerning the relationship between consciousness of the outer and consciousness of the inner.

Roughly twenty-five years ago I was invited to address a conference whose theme was "Dealing with the Gifted Child." The opening statement of my address was something like: "Ladies and gentlemen, parents and teachers, if you will go back in memory into your own childhood and connect with what you longed for from adults and perhaps did not get, you will know what the children entrusted to your care need from you." Then I went on to talk about what it was like to be a child, and what are often a child's frustrations, and what are a child's legitimate needs, in such a way as to stimulate the flow of feeling and memory within my listeners. I was aware that when we are hurt as children we often turn off, repress feeling, to make life bearable. Years later, when we have children of our own, childhood can seem an incomprehensible world. The result is that we are badly hampered in our efforts to see what needs to be seen and do what needs to be done. We are blind to the child we once were—and blind to the child in front of us. The problem is, more often than not we do not know we are blind. For this reason, I knew that empathy had to begin with self-awareness—with our inner reality and with the remembered experience of our own childhood. And in the discussion following my presentation, I was heartened to witness the number of spontaneous insights concerning what actions to take that members of the audience began sharing. In recalling what they had needed as children, they began to understand better what other children need.

I must add that while self-awareness was necessary, it was not all these parents and teachers required. Since every human being is unique, they needed to listen to these children and learn from them what might be most helpful in any particular case. Otherwise, the danger would be of projecting one's own preferences onto a child whom they did not fit. They needed to integrate inner and outer awareness.

The next story took place a year or two earlier than the above incident. In my early forties, I decided I wanted to experience a form of body therapy known as structural integration (or, more popularly, "Rolfing," after the originator of the method, Ida Rolf). This process involves deep massage and manipulation of the muscle fasciae to realign the body in more appropriate relation to gravity, to correct imbalances caused by entrenched muscular contractions, and to open areas of blocked feeling and energy. When treatment is successful, it leads to a general freeing up of the capacity to feel, greater awareness of and sensitivity to one's own physical processes, improved overall coordination, superior balance, and increased energy. Not everyone gains these benefits to the same degree (or at all), but for me it was very much the right treatment at the right time in my development. I felt lighter than I had in years. I experienced a general deepening of self-awareness. I felt freer emotionally. I felt as if walls within myself had dissolved. And I had more energy. I was not surprised that I felt better. What did surprise me—what I was completely unprepared for—was the change in my perceptiveness concerning other people.

During this period I was leading a number of psychotherapy groups, and my clients volunteered that they could notice changes in me week by week as the Rolfing progressed. I had had very little formal training in working with the body in psychotherapy, yet I found I was now able to "read" bodies to a new and astonishing degree. Slight changes in facial expression or eye movements, shifts of posture, subtle variations in ways of standing or sitting, changes of skin color, alterations in breathing patterns— all suddenly seemed to convey volumes of information to me as clearly as articulate speech. It was as if, in becoming more transparent to myself, I had shifted to a space that allowed others to become more transparent to me. For me, this was something of a revelation.

▲▲▲

**When we are able to see the internal more
clearly, we become able to see the external
more clearly.**

▼

What both of these stories are meant to illuminate is that when we are able to see the internal more clearly, we are able to see the external more clearly.

Now, by way of completing this discussion of the foundations of living consciously, I want to say a few words about the nature of reason and rationality.

REASON: THE NONCONTRADICTORY
INTEGRATION OF EXPERIENCE

On the morning of the day I began to write this section, I turned on the news while having breakfast, and the first item to come up on the screen was astronaut Jim Lovell being interviewed about his extraordinary experiences on Apollo 13. The film *Apollo 13,* based on his book *Lost Moon,* was about to be released. In a quietly understated way, Lovell told of the explosion of an oxygen tank that turned the mission into a race for survival against one potential catastrophe after another—from a rapidly diminishing supply of breathable air to a battery strength insufficient for a return to earth—in a deteriorating spacecraft hurtling through the cosmos to almost certain destruction. What was thrilling about the interview was the sense one got of the magnificent teamwork between the men on board the spacecraft and the support crew on earth interacting at a height of disciplined intelligence and passionate competence—which resulted in the craft and its inhabitants being brought safely home.

I thought—with acutely painful longing—of what it would be like to live in a world in which human beings functioned as a way of life as the people functioned in that crisis. I am referring not necessarily to the speed of response or sense of urgency that characterized that situation, but rather to the level of consciousness, rationality, and reliability the individuals involved exhibited. It was a marvel of integrated human efforts made possible only by the intransigent self-responsibility of every participant. I do not know how rational any of those people were in the rest of their lives, but in this situation, reality was an absolute (no one imagined the problem would go away if they simply didn't think about it), reason was an absolute (no one phoned his astrologer for suggestions), and the relationship between rationality and survival was understood by all.

If one wanted to see the spirituality of reason in action, I thought, this was it.

By "spiritual," I mean pertaining to consciousness (as contrasted with "material," which means pertaining to or constituted of matter); and further, pertaining to the needs and development of consciousness. In speaking of "the spirituality of reason" in this context, I wish to draw attention to the very high level at which consciousness is operating when individuals working at breath-stopping speed integrate and apply enormous abstractions from physics, chemistry, physiology, and any number of other sciences to arrive at immediate solutions to devastatingly difficult technological challenges—with the result that human beings survived who otherwise would have perished.

Among the many crimes committed against the younger generation, one of the worst is that young people are taught next to nothing about reason, rationality, or the importance of critical thinking. In a decent educational system, no one would graduate from high school who had not been taught the basic principles of logic or been trained to recognize logical fallacies. Children need to be taught not *what* to think but *how* to think. They need to be educated in the achievements of mind throughout history—and helped to understand that their ability to reason is what makes them uniquely human. They need help in understanding that their most precious asset is what they carry between their ears.

▲▲▲

Among the many crimes committed against
the younger generation, one of the worst is
that young people are taught next to nothing
about reason, rationality, or the importance of
critical thinking.

▼

No other gift to a young person could equal that of teaching the intimate relationship that exists between rationality and self-esteem—between consciousness and efficacy. This relationship has been a central theme of my writing for over three decades. If the essence of self-esteem is the experience of being competent to face the challenges of life, and if our mind is our basic tool of survival and of adaptation to reality, then no virtue is nobler or more practical than the appropriate exercise of mind.

Life existed on this planet for millions of years before a life form evolved from which, at a certain point in its development, the capacity to reason emerged. As a distinct human faculty and process, reason was identified explicitly and conceptually only about 2600 years ago, in ancient Greece. Approximately two centuries later, Aristotle defined man as "the rational animal." The definition did not mean that people always behaved rationally. It meant that the ability to reason (at least in its full form) was unique to our species. It was the trait that most distinguished our species from all others—and that made it possible to understand the greatest number of our actions and achievements.

To be moved by impulses we do not understand is not an exclusively human prerogative; lower animals live this way as a matter of course. But to assess and integrate the messages coming to us from our body, our emotions, our past knowledge, our imagination, external reality, and perhaps the experience of millions who have gone before us is a uniquely human capability—called thinking.

To have a brain and nervous system that automatically learns to retain and integrate disparate sensations (energy pulsations) so as to make possible the perception of solid objects is not an exclusively human trait; other animals are similarly endowed. But to integrate percepts into concepts, to identify certain aspects of reality, grasp the essentials they have in common, and integrate them into wider conceptual categories—then to do the same with one's concepts, integrating them into wider concepts or forming certain narrower concepts as subcategories of wider ones, building an increasingly complex structure of knowledge, bringing more and more of reality under the control of one's mind—so that one can build skyscrapers, devise sophisticated instruments for medical diagnosis, invent new ways to produce more and better with diminishing expenditures of energy, send men to the moon and bring them home safely—*that* is a possibility of our species alone, through the operation of our rational faculty.

One of the unique characteristics of our form of consciousness is that it is *self-reflexive*—meaning that mind can examine its own processes. We can ask, How did I arrive at that conclusion? Do I really know my reasons? Am I being influenced by prejudice? Do I have grounds to believe this is true, or do I merely *want* it to be true? Am I being logical right now? Do my conclusions really follow from my premises? We can monitor not only our mental operations but virtually any aspect of our existence. We can ask: Who am I? What do I want? Where am I going? For what purpose should I live? Are my actions in alignment with that purpose? Am I proud of my choices and decisions? To live consciously is necessarily to be concerned with such questions, and it is our rational faculty—our ability to think, and even to think about thinking—that makes such questions possible. A less evolved consciousness does not and cannot question its operations. A dog does not wonder if it is being swayed by inappropriate considerations. A chimpanzee does not ask itself if its goals are rational.

Since reason is understood many different ways by people, I need to develop a bit more fully the broad, universal sense in which I use the term.

Reason (or rationality) is the faculty that grasps relationships. It is the faculty that makes distinctions and looks for connections, that abstracts and unites, that differentiates and integrates. Reason generates general principles from concrete facts (induction), applies general principles to concrete facts (deduction), and relates new knowledge and information to our existing context of knowledge. Its guide is the law of noncontradiction.

▲ ▲ ▲

We must *choose* to think. ₆

▼

Observe that integration is central not only to the operation of mind but to every aspect of the life process. The growth of a fetus into a human being is a series of progressive stages of differentiation and integration. And any organism, human or otherwise, is a complex integrate of hierarchically organized structures and functions. We sustain ourselves physically by taking materials from the environment, breaking them down, reorganizing them, and achieving a new integration that converts these materials into the means of our survival. We can observe an analogous phenomenon in what we do cognitively. Just as integration is the cardinal principle of life, so it is the cardinal principle of mind. This principle is operative when, in the brains of humans or animals, sensations are retained and integrated (by nature's "programming") in such a way as to produce a perceptual awareness of entities—an awareness that humans and animals require for their survival. Integration is at the heart of the process of forming concepts and generating abstract thought—that is, the process of gaining knowledge on which distinctively *human* survival depends.

This process, of course, is not automatic. It is volitional—in contrast to perception, which *is* automatic. We must *choose* to think. At the conceptual level, we must *guide* and *monitor* our mental processes. We must check our conclusions against all available evidence—that is, we must reason.[6]

Reason is an evolutionary development. It is the instrument of awareness raised to the *conceptual* level. It is the power of integration inherent in life made *explicit* and *self-conscious.*

Rationality, which is the exercise of reason in judgment and action, should not be confused, as it so often is, with what people of a given time or place represent as the "reasonable." Many an innovator has been denounced as "unreasonable" for refusing to play by someone else's rules or to accept the "received wisdom" of his or her time. Often, rationality must challenge and reject what others call "reasonable."

On the most personal level, growing up, a young person of some independence questions many of the views handed out by elders. "Why?" he or she asks. "Why do you say that? What are your grounds?" And if satisfactory answers are not forthcoming, those views are not accepted merely because others describe them as "reasonable." One of the most precious traits of young people is the desire to understand, to make sense of things. This is the voice of reason within them.

▲ ▲ ▲

The quest of reason—this can hardly be stated often enough—is for *the noncontradictory integration of experience.*

▼

Historically, if some notion of the reasonable is overthrown by new evidence or more precise thinking, people sometimes say, "So much for reason." But it was the mistaken notion that was overthrown, not reason; indeed, reason was the instrument of the overthrow. The quest of reason—this can hardly be stated often enough—is for *the noncontradictory integration of experience.* This implies one's openness and availability to experience. Reason is the servant neither of tradition nor consensus.

This distinction between reason (or rationality) as a process and what some person or group labels "the reasonable" is of the highest importance. Much nonsense about the alleged "inadequacies" of reason is made possible by the failure to make this distinction.

It goes without saying that we are fallible. With the best will in the world, we can still make mistakes. But reason—in the global sense in which I define it here—offers us the possibility of self-correction. That is one of its unique characteristics. Other alleged paths to knowledge, such as faith or feeling, do not share this possibility; that is, they lack an inbuilt self-correcting dynamism.

Sometimes they may disclose a truth, sometimes not, but they have no internal means to distinguish, no internal standard by which to detect error or guide the way to its correction.

Apart from what we have already observed about our ability to monitor and assess our own mental operations, consider the following: Any time we review a plan we have made—in our personal life or in business—and spot an omission or oversight or unwarranted inference or some other kind of flaw in our thinking, and take steps to revise our plan, reason is operating in its self-correcting mode. Any time we change our mind about something, in response to new evidence or a new argument, thinking is used to revise thinking. Any time we are about to agree to a deal or proposal of some kind, and some signal of discomfort in our body or sense of static in our brain arrests our attention and makes us pause and check further—because experience has taught us not to ignore signals of that kind, even if we don't fully understand them —it is an act of rationality that is protecting us and impelling us to look again before we leap. (Regarding this last example, the role of reason is not always obvious to people; they may merely tell themselves, "I had a hunch." But it is reason that says, "Based on experience, better check this out." Or: "If the deal is so great, why do I feel uneasy? There's something here that doesn't 'compute,' something I can't integrate.")

▲ ▲ ▲

The practice of living consciously entails an openness to evidence that might suggest an error in one's thinking—and a willingness to correct such errors.

▼

Further, when we argue for some viewpoint and there is a gap or a flaw in our thinking and someone calls our attention to the error, it is reason that alerts us to the need to rethink our position. When new evidence is incompatible with (cannot be integrated with) our established views, it is reason that tells us we have to go back to the drawing board. If an event transpires that our belief system says is impossible, it is reason that instructs us to reexamine our premises.

The practice of living consciously entails an openness to evidence that might suggest an error in one's thinking—and a willingness to correct such an error. It is the opposite of self-defensive mental rigidity. Defensiveness is unconsciousness protecting itself. If we are invested in the fallacious notion that we must never make a mistake or that it is a reflection on our worth to admit an error, then we are driven to shrink our awareness—to induce blindness. Living consciously (and authentic self-esteem) require eagerness to discover one's errors and candor about admitting them. The underlying premise of this attitude is: I do not treat reality as an antagonist.

The self-correcting dynamism of reason is not automatic or instantaneous, given the facts of free will, human inertia, and the passion with which reason can be resisted. But eventually, reason and reality win. The progress of science and technology is a monument to this truth. (That technology may not always be used wisely or in the service of life is not a failure of reason but a failure in the exercise of reason; reason must be applied to ends, not only to means. I am strongly opposed to the notion of "instrumental reason," which confines rationality to the selection of means while claiming that ends are "outside reason." That the gas ovens of Nazi death camps operated efficiently does not make them expressions of human rationality. Reason does not permit the ignoring of context—that is, considering single events as if they occurred in a vacuum. Indeed, the practice of looking at events in their full context and assessing them accordingly is one of the hallmarks of rationality.) With regard to advances in science, note what generates the need for a new paradigm to replace an older one: the accumulation of new data that simply cannot be integrated into the older model or picture of reality. The battle cry of reason is "Integrate, integrate, integrate!" The drive to do so is the motor of scientific progress.

Of course, it would be a mistake to identify reason exclusively with science. Science is the rational, systematic study of the facts of reality; its aim is to discover laws of nature, to achieve a comprehensive, integrated knowledge that will make the universe intelligible. Science is an expression of reason, but it is not equivalent in meaning. Reason is the broader, more inclusive concept. One can be rational without being scientific—witness the everyday thinking we do that keeps our life flowing, such as meeting the challenges of our job or understanding, through conversation, aspects of one another's inner worlds.

To recognize the profoundly important role of reason in our lives is not to imply that reasoning is our only useful or legitimate mental activity. Fantasizing, daydreaming, creative mental playfulness, meditative self-observation, contemplative practices, nonlinear, nonverbal forms of "right hemisphere" cognition—all have profoundly useful roles, serve important purposes, and represent appropriate operations of mind. But it takes an act of thought to know when to let go of purposeful thinking and shift to another mode of mental functioning. And it is a function of reason to check the results of our mental operations against the full context of our knowledge. Precisely because its task is integration, reason is the ultimate umpire.

As philosopher Mortimer J. Adler rightly observes:

> *Of all the serious misfortunes that can befall us while we are alive and not threatened by terminal illness, the most grievous is loss of mind or, more specifically, loss of our intellectual power—our power of rational thought. . . .*
>
> *Deprivation of sight or hearing, partial paralysis of muscles, loss of limbs, even the conceptual blindness that is agnosia—all these misfortunes, however disabling, still allow us to live on the distinctly human plane. . . . But deprived of our intellectual minds, we are deprived of our humanity.*[7]

Many misunderstandings surround the idea of reason, and it is not possible to address them all here. But there are one or two more observations I need to make.

Many years ago, I noticed that when I wish to deepen my understanding of my client's feelings and emotional context, if I sit as my client is sitting, breathe as my client is breathing, and imagine myself somehow spiritually merging with my client (even though I cannot fully explain in words just how I am doing this), I find myself understanding the client in a new and deeper way, as evidenced by the insights that occur to me and by the responses I elicit. "But isn't this a nonrational form of knowledge?" colleagues have asked me. My answer is, not at all. I have never asserted that all our ideas can come to us only through a process of reasoning. Einstein, for example, spoke of the role of muscle sense in his theorizing. Nor have I ever insisted that we already possess full and comprehensive knowledge of all the ways in which one can access information about the universe. But it is reason, it is reality-testing, that can convert these possible insights into *knowledge*. We need reality-testing to verify that our insights represent facts.

▲ ▲ ▲

**One of the meanings of living consciously is:
Pay attention to what works, and do more of
it, and try to understand the principles
involved. And also: Pay attention to what
doesn't work, *and stop doing it.***

▼

Regarding the process I describe with clients in therapy, I can explain in part why it tends to be successful, but I cannot explain it entirely—not to my satisfaction. However, if I discover time and again that the method yields deeper awareness of my client's inner state, as confirmed by the client's feedback, then it is utterly reasonable to use this method as a tool. I do not assume it is infallible but, rather, continue to check its accuracy through further dialogue and observation.

It is reasonable to use a method that has a record of producing worthwhile results, even if we cannot account fully for why the method works. For thousands of years, people used folk remedies without understanding how or why they worked, and it would have been irrational not to, after observing the remedy's effectiveness.

One of the meanings of living consciously is: Pay attention to what works, and do more of it, and try to understand the principles involved. And also: Pay attention to what doesn't work *and stop doing it.*

REASON AND EMOTION: CHALLENGING THE NECESSITY FOR CONFLICT

One misunderstanding concerning reason has haunted mankind virtually since reason was first identified, and that is the relation of reason to emotion. A long tradition sees thought and feeling as adversaries. Traditionally, from the time of ancient Greece, the champions of thought saw emotions as "wild horses" that reason must subdue and control—while champions of feeling saw reason as a repressive force that obstructed the deep wisdom of blood and heart. As we will see later in this book, both these views are wrong, and both undermine the practice of living consciously.

Living consciously requires a rejection of this dichotomy and the mistaken premises underlying it. Living consciously entails the attainment of a wider field of vision that permits reason and emotion to be integrated rather than mutually opposed.

We will see that to feel honestly and deeply is to liberate the process of thinking clearly. To think clearly is to create a context for a passionate life. To live consciously is to rise above the view of the human spirit as a battlefield of conflicting forces and to see not war but harmony as the natural condition of an enlightened mind.

43

2

Choice and Responsibility

FOR many years, my wife Devers and I had a running problem that I failed to resolve. In the morning, when I made myself toast and coffee, I often spilled coffee on the kitchen floor. Not noticing I had done so, I did not clean it up. Devers would periodically point this out to me and ask me to be more careful. I would promise to do so and genuinely felt I had earnest intentions—but somehow I kept spilling coffee. At times I was flabbergasted when this was pointed out to me; I could not understand how or why it kept happening, despite my resolutions to be careful.

We had many discussions on this subject, some of them warm and friendly, but not all. I liked drinking coffee out of a mug, disliked bothering with saucers, and could not for the life of me understand why it was so difficult to balance the mug—as I kept explaining to an increasingly frustrated and baffled Devers.

The problem became acute when we built a new home and now had a much finer kitchen, with a white floor and white grouting. Cleaning coffee stains out of grouting can be a project, as I was to discover.

One day I was sitting at my computer when I heard Devers calling from the kitchen: *"Nathaniel!"* Pointing to coffee stains on the kitchen floor, Devers asked, in a tone of exasperation, "Is there any reason why it is *I* who should clean this up?"

"Absolutely not, darling," I answered. "I'll take care of it." On my knees with a damp sponge, I struggled to remove the stains from the grouting and finally remarked, "Gee, this is hard."

"There's cleanser under the sink," Devers answered. As I went to work with the cleanser, I heard Devers saying to my back, "I really don't know what to do about this. It's so frustrating. We've had a million conversations, and it keeps happening." Once again I proceeded to tell her how bewildered I was that the problem was still with us, no matter how often I told myself to be careful.

I did not learn until later that while Devers watched me, on my hands and knees, removing the last of the coffee stains, she was trying hard not to laugh. I thought she was still angry and that she was quite justified.

Then her expression changed to one of humor and triumph, and she announced, "I know how we're going to solve this. I'm going to adapt a technique I once saw Nathaniel Branden use in psychotherapy." When I heard that, I knew I was in trouble.

"Are we agreed," she asked me, "that you should not spill coffee?"

I answered, "Of course."

"And are we agreed," she went on, "that you are *physically able* not to spill coffee?"

Again I said, "Of course."

Devers then said, "Okay, I want your word that any time I find spilt coffee on the floor, you will owe me five hundred dollars."

"Five hundred dollars. Isn't that extreme?"

"So is your spilling coffee for seventeen years."

Through a long moment of silence I stared at the knowledge that she was absolutely right and that what she was proposing was reasonable. I felt that in all logic and justice I had to shake her hand on this deal.

Back in my office, with a rising sense of desperation, I thought that now I really had to solve this problem. I could not afford to pay Devers thirty-five hundred dollars a week for the luxury of being absent-minded (sometimes this is a polite word for semi-unconscious). So I asked myself questions I had not thought of asking myself before: *Why* did I spill my coffee? What made *not* spilling it so difficult? And suddenly the answer was clear to me: I spilt coffee because I always filled the cup to the very top. If I only filled the cup to the three-quarters mark, it would be simple to avoid spilling coffee. And since I never drink more than half a cup anyway . . .

From that day, I stopped spilling coffee.

The moral of the story is, there is operating consciously and there is *operating consciously.* Certainly I would have said I was being adequately conscious in my efforts to solve the spilt coffee problem. But when suddenly the stakes for failing were raised to another level, my efforts acquired a new urgency and I directed a more intense awareness at the problem than I previously had done. I had been conscious, of course, but I *became more conscious.*

▲ ▲ ▲

**Do I take responsibility for generating a level
of awareness appropriate to the context? Do I
give my activities the best consciousness of
which I am capable, or do I settle for
something less than that?**

▼

At my earlier level of consciousness, I wanted to solve the problem, no doubt, but at some level I was *willing* for the problem not to be solved *immediately:* the determination to correct the situation was less than absolute. When the determination became absolute, I raised my consciousness—and found the solution.

For the reader who is curious as to what Devers might have

done differently at the very beginning to prevent this problem from remaining unresolved so long, I will add the following: If I had been consulted about such a problem, I would have suggested to the wife, after her first few discussions with her husband failed to produce a change in his behavior, that she stop cleaning up after him and that instead she call him into the kitchen and say simply, "Here is a spilt coffee spot that needs cleaning up." I promise you he would have stopped spilling coffee in much less than seventeen years.

However, to return to the incident as it actually happened: what I had to be willing to look at later, and this was challenging, was the fact that the knowledge that I was agitating Devers with my spilt coffee was not—evidently—a powerful enough motivater in itself to generate change. So I was drawn down to a deeper level of self-examination on this score.

The point here is that consciousness can operate at higher and lower levels of clarity and intensity, and in any given situation, the question is not whether I am conscious or not in the literal sense but whether I bring to the occasion the level of consciousness I require to be effective.

Or, to put it another way: Do I take responsibility for generating a level of awareness appropriate to the context?

The example I have given is mundane. But the principle involved is the same whether the issue is as basic as not spilling coffee or as complex as raising children, running a corporation, or writing a book. Do we give our activities the best consciousness of which we are capable, or do we settle for something less than that?

The question of living consciously would not even arise if we did not have the power, within limits, to regulate the activity of our mind—that is, if consciousness were not volitional. A being whose consciousness functioned automatically would not need to be advised to live consciously. No alternative would be perceived to exist. A dog is, in effect, programmed by nature to use its senses optimally. We are not programmed to use our minds optimally. We may or may not choose to do the thinking our goals and well-being require. The decision is left to us. The ability to focus our mind or not to, to think or not to, to strive for awareness or not to, to face reality or not to, is our free will.

To live consciously, we must understand the nature of our choice in the matter—that is, our freedom and responsibility.

FREE WILL: THE CHOICE TO TURN
CONSCIOUSNESS BRIGHTER OR DIMMER

The essence of our psychological freedom may be summarized as follows:

We are free to focus our mind, or not to bother, or to actively avoid focusing.

We are free to think, or not to bother, or to actively avoid thinking.

We are free to strive for greater clarity with regard to some issue confronting us, or not to bother, or to actively seek darkness.

We are free to examine unpleasant facts or to evade them.

The process of focusing our mind consists, in effect, of giving ourselves the order, in relation to some issue, "Grasp this." Suppose, for example, we face a desktop full of work needing to be completed, and initially we are in a somewhat vague and poorly focused mental state. Then we sigh, take a deep breath, pick up some document, and in effect tell ourselves, "Grasp this. See where you left off, re-create your context, grasp what the situation now requires—and proceed." In that instant, we shift into clearer focus and higher consciousness.

▲ ▲ ▲

The choice to think is the choice to rise from
the sensory-perceptual level and the awareness

**of moods, feelings, or floating mental images
to the active, *conceptual* level of consciousness.**

▼

Everyone is familiar with experiences of this kind—just as everyone is familiar with the opposite experience, where we elect to remain in an unfocused state and avoid the reality confronting us and also avoid thinking about the consequences of our avoidance.

The choice to think is the choice to rise from the sensory-perceptual level and the awareness of moods, feelings, or floating mental images to the active, *conceptual* level of consciousness. In other words, it is the choice to pursue some goal entailing differentiation and integration, abstraction and concretization—so as to gain increased mastery over some domain of concern to us.

The choice not to bother, or to actively avoid thinking, is the choice to remain stuck at the level of sensory awareness and passive feeling in relation to whatever it is we are not dealing with. In such a case, we evade the fact that something requires our attention and we drift mentally, resort to alibis and rationalizations, change the subject, or get suddenly sleepy—seeking one escape route or another away from the challenge we do not choose to face.

Consider a situation at work where someone tells us of a problem in our organization. Suppose we do not want the responsibility of having to deal with it, even though that responsibility is properly ours. So at first we have great difficulty understanding what is being said to us, then in remembering it, then in grasping what needs to be done. Artfully, we summon not clarity but confusion into our consciousness. "Confusion" is our defense against thought and responsibility. Or the problem might not concern work but, rather, our marriage or an issue with our children, and we prefer to avoid rather than confront—so we call on the same strategy of self-induced "confusion." In the workplace and our personal life, this strategy is common. If we are aware of this pattern and wish to break out of it, the most relevant question to ask is, "What am

49

I pretending not to know?" Asking that question implies, of course, that we have already begun shifting to a clearer, more focused level of consciousness—and this is an act of choice.

In any situation we confront the issue: Shall I or shall I not strive for awareness, clarity, understanding? And the way we build confidence in our mind and gain increasing control over our life is by repeatedly responding in the affirmative. We make a muscle strong by using it. We make a mind strong the same way. This point is essential to learning how to grow in self-esteem.

However, consciousness is necessarily selective. We cannot be aware of everything. The choice to focus in one direction is, in effect, the choice not to focus in other directions. The choice to think about one subject is the choice, in that moment, not to think about something else. If I am listening to what you are saying, I am choosing to screen out the conversation at the next table or the traffic sounds from the street. If I suddenly hear an explosion outside the restaurant, I may orient my attention toward the outside and withdraw my attention from our conversation.

This leads us to the issue of consciousness and context.

CONTEXT DETERMINES WHAT STATE OF CONSCIOUSNESS IS APPROPRIATE

Generally speaking, it is our actions, values, and goals that determine what is the appropriate mind-state in any particular situation. Right now, I have given myself the assignment of writing about consciousness and context. That purpose keeps me focused on the issues we have been discussing and the steps needed to develop my points clearly.

At the same time, I am vaguely aware of the shouting and laughing sounds of two of our visiting grandchildren who are playing in the swimming pool; I think it would be enjoyable to get up from my computer and join them, but then I think that I would like to complete this section as rapidly as possible—so I pull my mind back to the task at hand. As I continue to write, the sounds recede in my conscious awareness. Very little has the power to reach me now but the thoughts rising in my mind or forming on the screen in front of me. My concentration is so intense I am almost in a trance state. That state is appropriate right now. It serves my purpose.

But I know that later, when I join my wife and grandchildren for dinner, I will need to leave this state and shift to another. If I persisted in this state at the dinner table, six-year-old Jordan might say to me, "Grandpa, where are you?" Or ten-year-old Ashley might say, "Grandpa, are you still at your computer?" When I am with my grandchildren, I choose to be present to the encounter. I want to be conscious of what is taking place between us. So the object of my focus changes and also the nature of my mental activity: I will not be so oriented to abstract thought but will rather be oriented primarily to seeing and hearing and feeling. That will serve my new purpose, which is to fully experience my grandchildren and the pleasure of their company.

Let us say that later, while the children are being put to bed, I go to my office—perhaps to meditate. I have no other purpose in this new context than to achieve for a while an experience of inner stillness. I am aware this may be refreshing or lead to the inspiration of some new idea for the book, but I am not focused on or attached to possible consequences of that kind. All I want is the experience of stillness. Let whatever happens happen; and if nothing noteworthy happens, this is acceptable. While sitting quietly, I suddenly remember that on my desk is a contract I have to study —and I start thinking about it. In this context, given my purpose, that is not appropriate, does not serve me. So I let go of concern with the contract and reenter stillness.

Some time later, perhaps before retiring, I decide to take a look at the contract. Now I engage in a kind of mental activity significantly different from what I was doing when writing, talking with my grandchildren, or sitting quietly (although there is some overlap with the mental processes involved in writing). Now my mind is set to the assignment of considering everything that might be relevant to this contract; above all, I am concerned with the implications of the statements I am reading and what is or is not covered.

Let us say that still later I am in bed making love with my wife. The mental activity is again different. I am not developing a thesis, not creating, not analyzing, not meditating, and probably not talking much, either. Yet I am fully aware, in the way I need to be for the purpose of the encounter, which is physical and emotional intimacy.

One factor will be present to all these activities, if I am operating consciously. I will be present to what I am doing. And I will be generating an awareness appropriate to the occasion. In one context, a very abstract kind of awareness is called for; in another, a high sensory awareness is appropriate. Neither is right nor wrong in a vacuum. It depends on my context, including my purpose.

▲ ▲ ▲

Context determines what mind-state is appropriate.

▼

But if we are to operate consciously, there needs to be congruence between what we are physically doing, what our goal or purpose is, and our mind-state. When there is lack of congruence, we are ineffective. If I retained the mental operations appropriate to lovemaking while trying to write this passage—or the mental operations appropriate to writing while making love—either way, the results would be unfortunate. The principle is: context determines what mind-state is appropriate.

▲ ▼ ▲

When we act, there is a great deal that we wisely and properly leave unconscious. It is in the nature of human learning that we automate new knowledge and skills, such as speaking a language or driving an automobile, so that they do not continue to require of us the level of explicit awareness necessary during the learning stage. As mastery is attained, they drop into the accumulated repertoire of the subconscious, thus freeing the conscious mind for the new and unfamiliar. Living consciously does not mean we retain in explicit awareness everything we ever learned, which would be neither possible nor desirable. Learning to ski, I had to be highly conscious of the smallest movements of my feet, legs, hips, and shoulders. Doing so improved my skiing, but if I focused too much on those movements now, it would impede the smoothness of my skiing. However, if I want an instructor to give me pointers on improving my technique, I might have to focus on those movements again. If we want to be effective, we need to learn what to pay attention to and what to leave "on automatic." Again, we can never say what is or is not operating consciously until we know the context.

▲ ▲ ▲

**If we want to be effective, we need to learn
what to pay attention to and what to leave "on
automatic."**

▼

STRATEGIES OF AVOIDANCE

When we seek escape from consciousness, the usual motives are fatigue, laziness, fear, pain, or the desire to indulge inappropriate wishes.

The first motive is not ordinarily dangerous and is easily remediable by getting some rest. The other motives can be dangerous, and we will examine them below. But first, let us consider not *why* we avoid awareness but *how* we do so. What is our mind doing when we are backing away from something we need to confront or examine?

The simplest strategy of avoidance consists of giving up the effort to direct the flow of awareness. We abandon purpose. We surrender to passive drifting. We let ourselves be carried along by mental associations. Our mind becomes a ship without anyone at the helm. This state is not an unnatural one; all of us spend some time in it—not necessarily out of an impulse to avoid but merely as a form of resting, and there are times when this is quite appropriate. It is what we do when our intention is to fall asleep. But if we shifted into that state while a teacher was telling us that one of our children was in major trouble, while a spouse was telling us our relationship was in crisis, or while a customer or supervisor was expressing serious dissatisfaction with our performance—if we surrendered to passivity precisely when we needed the clearest thinking of which we were capable—that would be operating unconsciously.

Another form of consciousness avoidance (reality avoidance) is passive surrender to the feeling or emotion of the moment in a way that effectively freezes any rational mental activity. Fear, pain, anger, or some other emotion become one's whole universe, bigger than oneself. This is entirely different from being a conscious witness to one's feelings, experiencing them in full clarity with the intention of understanding and possibly transcending them. This is mindless submergence in feeling, a state in which nothing can be learned.

This could be the short-term condition of anyone if the emotion were powerful enough to temporarily stop thought. But for a rational mind, this would be a state to be overcome—not indulged and even embraced.

It is certainly possible to feel intensely and at the same time retain the clarity of one's thinking. I do not wish to suggest an *intrinsic* dichotomy between emotion and consciousness. Yet it is easy enough to observe that for many people, feelings and emotions are principally a refuge from reality. It is where they go to hide out. They act on the premise that as long as they stay absorbed in the fear, pain, anger, or desire, they do not have to think, do not have to perceive, do not have to connect, do not have to act responsibly. I am afraid—let the world stop. I am in pain—let someone do something. I am angry—let no one dare reproach me or challenge me about anything. I want—let reality keep out of my way. In this mind-state, feelings and emotions equal unconsciousness.

Yet another avoidance strategy consists of switching one's mind away from where it needs to be to some irrelevant (in the context) issue—from blaming to alibiing to rationalizing to intellectualizing to clowning and cracking jokes to any form of mental busywork that can hold reality at bay. Or perhaps the flight might be into action. Suddenly one must get to one's desk. Or do something charitable. Or visit one's mother. Or clean one's tennis shoes (during a snowy winter).

Psychologically, what is being avoided in all such cases is consciousness. Existentially, what is being avoided is reality.

AGAINST CONSCIOUSNESS: MOTIVES FOR FLIGHT FROM AWARENESS

Exercising focused consciousness is mental work and requires an effort. This, for some people, is enough of a deterrent right there. When I first wrote about this phenomenon in *The Psychology of Self-Esteem,* I called it "anti-effort." Today I prefer to describe it as the problem of laziness.

▲▲▲
**Passivity as a policy leaves us feeling
incompetent in the face of too many of life's
challenges and opportunities. It also leaves us
with underdeveloped self-esteem.**
▼

"Laziness" does not sound like a very serious psychological term, yet I no longer think we can adequately account for human behavior without this concept. There is such a thing as a simple disinclination to exert effort. All of us are familiar with it. All of us succumb to it at least occasionally. If we permit ourselves to do so now and again, either as a legitimate form of rest or a short-term self-indulgence, with no intention of permanently avoiding what we know we need to consider—then ordinarily no harm is done. But as a way of life, as a persistent response, such a policy is self-destructive. Passivity as a policy leaves us feeling incompetent in the face of too many of life's challenges and opportunities. It also leaves us with underdeveloped self-esteem.

Fear is another motive that we may permit to paralyze thought. As to what we might be afraid of, there are many possibilities. For example:

> Fear that our thinking will not prove correct—in other words, fear we might make an error; fear of our fallibility.

> Fear that if we act on our judgment and are wrong, it will be our fault—there will be no one to blame but ourselves, and others may hold us accountable.

> Fear of facing truths about ourselves (about our thoughts, feelings, or actions) we have been denying, avoiding, or disowning so as to protect our self-esteem or our pretense at it.

> Fear of facing truths about another person that, if acknowledged, might impel us to rock the boat of the relationship or even destroy it.

> Fear of not knowing how to deal with the realities one is acknowledging.

> Fear of being overwhelmed by one's inner world once one opens the door to it and of "losing one's mind" or losing all ability to cope with life.

> Fear of losing face in the eyes of significant others if certain truths about oneself are exposed, so that one dreads to expose them even to one's own inspection.

You might find it illuminating to pause for a moment and notice your own mental state and processes right now, in response to the above paragraphs. One friend who read a draft of this chapter wrote in the margin: "This is very powerful. I had a hard time staying conscious through it. I wanted to shut down."

To comment on each of these fears in turn:

It is not difficult to see that surrender to **the fear of one's fallibility** is self-destructive. One evades the fact that surrender to fear of choosing or deciding is itself a choice or a decision and will have consequences—like the executive who is afraid to exercise judgment and initiative in the face of rapid economic change and watches helplessly as his business loses market share to competitors.

▲ ▲ ▲

Whether in the workplace or in the sphere of personal relationships, success belongs to those who are willing to take responsibility for attaining their desires—those who respond to life proactively rather than passively, choosing independence over dependence.

▼

The same observation applies to surrender to **the fear of self-responsibility.** If our highest priority is not to achieve our goals but rather to avoid being blamed or held accountable, we are not going anywhere very rewarding or fulfilling in life. Our timidity becomes our prison. The dread we do not challenge sets the boundaries of our existence. Whether in the workplace or the sphere of personal relationships, success belongs to those who are willing to take responsibility for attaining their desires—those who respond to life proactively rather than passively, choosing independence over dependence.

▲ ▼ ▲

As to **facing truths about our own thoughts, emotions, and behavior,** anyone who has had any success with psychotherapy has almost certainly learned about the power of self-acceptance. When we can own and accept who we are; when we can make peace with the fact that our thoughts, emotions, and actions are expressions of self *at least at the time they occur;* when we can open ourselves to self-awareness; when we can drop judging in favor of seeing—we grow stronger and feel more whole. We are not obliged to like or condone everything we observe, but neither do we need to collapse into self-rejection. What clients in successful therapy discover is that, contrary to their notion that if they accept unwanted traits they will be permanently stuck with them, just the opposite is true: self-acceptance is the foundation of growth and change.

If I do not allow myself to know what I really think (or think in some context), if I deny and disown my thoughts when they feel embarrassing or troublesome, I cannot bring them into contact with the rest of my knowledge, cannot rationally process and perhaps grow beyond them, can only remain stuck with them. If I do not allow myself to know what I really feel (or feel in some context) and if I deny and disown any feelings or emotions that disturb my equilibrium or my self-concept, I repress vital information about my beliefs and values (of which the feelings and emotions are expressions). Therefore, I cannot learn from them, cannot revise them, and I can only go on being frightened any time they threaten to surface. If I do not allow myself to recognize and own actions that now distress me to remember, if I do not take responsibility for them as *mine,* what will prompt me to act differently in the future? I will have learned nothing.

▲ ▲ ▲

Self-acceptance is the foundation of growth and change.

▼

When we **evade the truth about those we deal with, for fear of disturbing the relationship,** we set ourselves up for inevitable suffering. If I am honest with myself about someone's shortcomings but choose to go on dealing with him or her because of other benefits, and therefore do not complain or express shock if the shortcomings express themselves, I am not engaged in evasion or self-deception. I am in effect taking a calculated risk based on what amounts to a cost-benefit analysis. But if I choose not to be conscious of plainly apparent dangers—if I deny or rationalize my spouse's abusiveness, pretend not to see evidence of infidelity, or, in business, make myself oblivious to the shortcomings of a deal because I want so much for the project to work—then I am inviting the pain and disappointment I will experience. I have forfeited the right to cry "betrayal." I have disarmed myself, and by my cooperation I have signaled my partner that his or her behavior is acceptable and there is no need or reason to change.

It is undeniable that if we commit to operating consciously, we may sometimes be confronted with realities we do not know how to deal with. For example, a couple lacking the communication skills that many educated people take for granted today might have no idea what to do when faced with a conflict in their relationship. So they may prefer to "bury" their issues (go unconscious concerning them) rather than bring them into clear, frightening focus. Such a decision is hardly incomprehensible, especially in earlier times in our history. And yet we know that their interests would be better served if they kept their perceptions unrepressed, even if they know of no remedial action to take and can only bear what they do not know how to change. The reason is that what we repress does not simply disappear; at an unconscious level, it remains active. It affects us in ways we do not recognize: we may become irritable, depressed, sick, or behave erratically. To protect against this, we do not need to stay focused on the negatives in our relationship—it would not serve any useful purpose and would in fact be dysfunctional—but we need to be aware of their existence.

▲ ▲ ▲

What we repress does not simply disappear; at
an unconscious level, it remains active.

▼

The fear that we will be overwhelmed and lose the ability to function if we permit ourselves to be "too conscious" has no basis

in reality. It is a concern I have heard most often from women who are frightened of their own anger. Sometimes, when their disowned rage begins to surface, they wonder if they are going "mad." If and when they permit themselves to confront their feelings—without acting on them in destructive ways but pursuing real solutions to their frustrations—they normally feel not less in control but more in control and more in balance. Whenever we are able to integrate a piece of the self that has been split off, the result is an increased sense of wholeness. However, if an individual has been protecting his or her equilibrium for many years by what I call "strategic unconsciousness," it is very difficult to come to this understanding without psychotherapy or a professional guide.

All the foregoing comments regarding fear as a motive for the avoidance of consciousness apply equally to pain as a motive. To pull back from pain is a normal response. If contemplating certain thoughts or memories stimulates suffering or anguish, one's impulse to withdraw consciousness is not abnormal. And such withdrawal is not necessarily undesirable—if no action needs to be taken and nothing further needs to be understood. Contemplation of the painful has no intrinsic merit. But often we avoid consciousness when we know there *are* actions we need to take and matters we *do* need to better understand. An example would be some error we have made that has had unfortunate consequences. We need to look at that error until we understand why we made it. We need to look at the consequences until we have accepted and fully integrated their reality. The value of such a policy is that it minimizes the likelihood of our making that error again. To a rational mind, pain is not a valid reason to go unconscious *when there are issues demanding attention.*

When a marriage or a business is failing, it may be very painful to look at the causes. But if they are not faced, neither learning nor changes in behavior are possible. If a child is in deep emotional trouble, it may be very painful for parents to confront the full reality of the situation. But if they refuse to, they are powerless to respond effectively. It may be very painful for me to identify how far I am from my aspirations. But if I don't, what will bring me closer to them?

Since our focus here is on the avoidance of pain, I want to stress that when I speak about the choice to operate consciously, I am referring to the domain of the volitional. Trauma—by which I mean a shock, terror, or pain beyond an individual's ability to absorb and integrate—can produce blocked areas within the psyche not accessible to ordinary efforts at awareness. Unconsciousness in this instance represents the organism's effort to protect itself. Professional assistance is usually required for dealing with problems of this kind, and such problems and their treatment are outside the scope of this discussion. We do not expect a person to operate more consciously in areas beyond his or her control, although a psychotherapist can often assist someone to extend the boundaries of control. So when I speak of an individual's need to operate with greater consciousness, I refer to contexts in which such a choice realistically exists.

▲ ▲ ▲
**People who are governed by a respect for
reality lead lives that work better than those of
people who place wishes above reason.**
▼

Finally, consider **the avoidance of reality in order to indulge desires reason cannot sanction** (such as going on a holiday at the cost of being unable to pay one's rent or practicing unprotected sex with a partner whose history is suspect). This is one of the commonest of all motives for suspending consciousness. It is also one of the commonest ways in which people create suffering for themselves. That which is, *is,* and our wishes do not obliterate the discomfiting facts we decline to consider. Against all our desires to the contrary, reality remains intransigent. When we attempt to defy (evade) reality, we sentence ourselves to anxiety—because at some level we know that, in life, it is reality and not our desires that has the last word. (What allows us to be deceived about this point is that other people sometimes protect us from the consequences of our irrationalities—not ultimately, perhaps, but in the short term.) If one looks beyond the range of the moment, it is not difficult to see that people governed by a respect for reality lead lives that work better than those of people who place wishes above reason.

▲▼▲

I would like to share a rather amusing story that illustrates what the avoidance of awareness can look like among a group of mental health professionals. I was conducting a seminar on working with self-esteem in psychotherapy. Sentence-completion work figures prominently in my method of therapy, and I wanted this group of psychotherapists to have some experience of its uses and possibilities. When working with an individual client, I provide a sentence stem—an incomplete sentence—and ask that the stem be repeated over and over again, with a different ending each time. Any ending is acceptable that is a grammatical completion of the sentence. In this case, however, working with a large group, I worked a little differently. I had the participants break up into subgroups of four or five. I would call out a stem, and one person in each subgroup would repeat it and add an ending; then the person to his or her right would repeat it and add an ending, then the next person, round and round, until I called out a new stem. In the course of forty-five minutes, I called out perhaps twenty incomplete sentences. Among them was the stem "Sometimes I get defensive when—"

I noticed that some people hesitated too long before completing a stem, and I encouraged them, as I always do, not to censor, not to worry about saying "the right thing" but to say anything, just so the sentence was completed. When participants are willing to do this and the material flows without editing or withholding, the results can be astonishing in terms of self-discovery, new integrations, and personal growth.

Later the entire class reassembled, and we discussed the exercise. The participants spoke enthusiastically about how much they had learned about themselves and one another during this process. Very casually, I observed that sometimes people had more difficulty with one stem than another, and I inquired whether anyone had noticed any stem that seemed tougher to work with.

There was total silence. No one responded. I waited a while, then encouraged the general discussion to continue.

A while later, making no reference to my earlier inquiry, I asked whether anyone had noticed in his or her subgroup that someone had more difficulty with one stem than another. And if so, what stem was it? Instantly, hands went up, and several students remarked, "In my group, it seemed to me that some people had trouble with the stem 'Sometimes I get defensive when—' "

I could not resist smiling. These mental health professionals could see the problem in others, but they evidently had difficulty seeing it in themselves. And even after I pointed it out, they were slow to absorb the significance of what had taken place—perhaps because it was hard on their self-image. If the incident was amusing, it was also a little disappointing. Given their profession, I had hoped for a bit more self-awareness of their own defensiveness.

"If we examine our own processes during this exercise," I suggested, "perhaps we will be better able to understand our clients."

Another story, not at all amusing, illustrates yet another aspect of both the challenges of living consciously and the nature of the sentence-completion process. I was conducting a weekend seminar based on *The Six Pillars of Self-Esteem*. After discussing for a while the idea of living consciously, I proposed the first exercise of the weekend. I asked the class to open notebooks and write an incomplete stem at the top of the page: "If I bring five percent more consciousness to my daily activities—" Then I asked them to write six to ten endings as rapidly as they could. Later, I asked for volunteers to share some of their endings. I heard such completions as "I would make fewer mistakes; I would get more accomplished; I would respect myself more; I would see more clearly what needs to be done;" and so on.

But one woman raised her hand and announced, "I couldn't do anything with this process. I just can't do sentence-completion work."

I have taught sentence completion to thousands of people and knew her statement to be untrue. I asked, "Do you understand that all you have to do is put down any ending that would grammatically complete the sentence?" When she said yes, I went on, "Would you be willing, right now, to give me one grammatical ending for that stem?" She responded by saying, "If I bring five percent more consciousness to my daily activities, I would see more." "Excellent," I said. "Could I have one more ending?" She answered, "—I would have to face tough issues." There was a pause. Then she said almost as an afterthought, "Well, actually, I did write down one ending before, when you first gave the exercise, and then I went blank." She looked at her notebook and read, "If I bring five percent more consciousness to my daily activities, I'll have to face the fact that I want to divorce my husband."

I paused, to allow her and the class to absorb this. Then I said, "Sometimes facing difficult issues can take a lot of courage."

She nodded. I thought her eyes looked clearer.

Addressing the class, I observed, "So the question is: Do we lead better, more fulfilling lives if we allow ourselves to know our unhappiness or if we don't? Which strategy allows us to be more effective?"

TO BE IN LOVE WITH LIFE ON EARTH

I trust it is clear that our discussion of consciousness is entirely this-worldly. It is directed at the needs and possibilities of earthly existence.

When we live consciously, we anchor spirituality in the challenges and opportunities of our uniquely human condition. We do not turn our back on life. We embrace it. And we will see that in doing so, we are led to embrace the continuing evolution of consciousness itself—because life is growth, motion, expansion, unfolding, a dynamic thrust forever transcending yesterday to reach tomorrow.

Some of what I say may evoke associations with the Buddhist concept of "mindfulness." To be sure, there are some areas of agreement here—for instance, the importance of being present to what we are doing. (And sometimes I speak of living mindfully as a synonym for living consciously.) But there are also differences that anyone familiar with Buddhism will recognize—for instance, I do not share the Buddhist view that self is an illusion (as I discuss in chapter 7).

In any event, with the context we have established, we are ready to address the issue, What does a life lived consciously look like? What does it entail?

3

A Conscious Life—1: Knowing What We Are Doing While We Are Doing It

IN this chapter and the next we will look at some of the key areas of everyday life from the perspective of the question: What would it mean to live consciously in this context?

To begin with, a few preliminary observations:

I have already identified the simplest application of mindfulness: being present to what I am doing while I am doing it. Stated in the negative, being present to what I am doing means *not* acting while my mind is somewhere else; *not* acting mechanically. Stated in the positive, it means acting in a mind-state appropriate to being effective. So if my child is talking to me about some hurtful situation, my focus will be on seeing, hearing, and being sensitive to the emotional subtext of the child's statements. If my computer teacher is explaining how some program works, my focus is more impersonal; however, if I am not present to what I am hearing and being shown, I am unlikely to grasp or retain what is being explained to me.

True, there are simple physical tasks we can perform without full mental attention and while carrying on another activity. We can rinse dishes and put them in the dishwasher while talking with someone. We can drive a car while listening to music. However, if we have an unfamiliar problem with the dishwasher, or if traffic difficulties suddenly arise, we pull our focus away from the conversation or the music and raise the level of consciousness we bring to the troublesome area. Or rather, this is what we do if we are basically in a mindful state. If we are, then at all times we remain present enough to recognize when greater attention is needed. Acting consciously requires not necessarily an exclusive focus on one thing but an *appropriate* focus—meaning one that allows us to respond effectively.

If we are present to what we are doing, we tend to be alert and sensitive to incoming information that bears on the situation with which we are dealing. Our consciousness is open to receive. Mentally, we are proactive rather than passive. In such circumstances we are not operating mechanically; that is, we are not running old automatized routines with no fresh participation of mind brought to the occasion. In this moment of time, we are alive in the full sense. Life is not happening while we are somewhere else.

▲ ▲ ▲

**If we are present to what we are doing, our
consciousness is open to receive.**

▼

Being present to what we are doing does not mean "being in the now" in a way that drops all connection to past and future. *Living consciously entails being in the present without losing the wider context.* The context is there as background, and what we are doing is foreground. Then we are *in* the moment but not *trapped* in the moment. This is the state that makes optimal action possible.

I stress this point because injunctions like "be here now" are sometimes interpreted (or misinterpreted) to mean a shrinking of awareness to encompass only the immediate moment, with the rest of one's knowledge cast into oblivion and with no concern for the future consequences of one's acts. The ultimate absurdity of this understanding of "be here now" is captured in the cartoon showing a man falling from a skyscraper who remarks in mid-flight, "So far, so good."

If the facts of reality were always to our liking, many people would find being present and living consciously easier and more pleasant than they do now. But the obvious truth is that sometimes we are obliged to confront and deal with facts we do not like at all. For some people, the appearance of a discomfiting fact is a signal to suspend consciousness and to (mentally) disappear. The implicit premise behind their avoidance is a self-deceiving subjectivism: What I don't choose to look at does not (for all practical purposes) exist. So, as I have already noted, implicit in living consciously is a policy of living *responsibly toward reality.*

In psychotherapy, when I raise the issue of being present to what we are doing, I sometimes give a client a sentence-completion exercise to help illuminate the issue. For instance, I might ask a client to keep repeating aloud endings for the sentence stem "If I were to be more present to what I am doing—" Typical endings include "I wouldn't make so many mistakes; I'd see more; I'd see things I might not want to see; my family would feel more visible to me; my children would feel heard; I'd get more done; I'd know what was going on; I'd be more aware of my emotions; I'd have to face what I was feeling; I'd feel stronger; at first I think I'd be more anxious; I'd feel I was living my life."

I might follow with the stem "The bad thing about being present to what I am doing is—" (The phrase "the bad thing" is an informal way to open a channel for expressing the negatives associated with being more present.) I typically hear such endings as "I'd feel apprehensive; I'd have to make things real; I couldn't hide; I couldn't deny; what if I see things I don't know how to deal with?; the thought of it makes me uncomfortable; I'd feel too much; I'd be too vulnerable; people could see me; my anxiety would go up; my anger might come out; I'd be out of control; it's too much of a responsibility; it's too hard; I couldn't escape."

▲ ▲ ▲

**Often, a flight from reality is a flight from the
reality of our inner state.**

▼

One of the themes one can notice in these endings is fear that, if we are present to what we are doing, emotions we have been denying or avoiding may rise to the surface of awareness and we will have to confront them. Often, a flight from the present is a flight from the reality of our inner state. This is not the only motive, to be sure, but in my experience it is one of the most common. Another, closely related, is fear of what we might see—for example, our negative feelings toward a parent, spouse, or child, or memories of past shameful actions we have taken—and fear of how we will feel about what we might see.

When we discuss the issue of living consciously, the question of intelligence often arises. But intelligence is not the issue here. We are not all equals in intelligence; a person of high intelligence has the potential to grasp things that are outside the range of a person of low intelligence. But intellectual ability is actually irrelevant—because when I speak of living consciously, it is always with reference to an individual's own capabilities. Is he or she operating mindfully within the limits of what is volitionally possible to that individual? A person of modest intellect does not become a professor of astrophysics, and so the question of whether or not he or she brings an appropriate level of consciousness to that job does not come up. It may, however, come up with regard to his or her clerical duties. The principle is, "From each according to his ability."

To live consciously means to seek to be aware of everything that bears on our actions, purposes, values, and goals—to the best of our ability, whatever that ability may be—and to behave in accordance with that which we see and know. This practice is applicable on any level of intelligence and is unaffected by the facts that a highly intelligent person may think of questions a less intelligent person will not and that the mind of the more intelligent person may embrace more of reality than the less intelligent. The only question relevant here is: Is the individual operating consciously *within his or her limits?* In the conduct of everyday life, a person of average IQ—a train conductor, let us say—may be operating more mindfully than a scientist with a genius IQ.

▲ ▲ ▲

**To live consciously means to seek to be aware
of everything that bears on our actions,
purposes, values, and goals—to the best of our
ability, whatever that ability may be—and to
behave in accordance with that which we see
and know.**

▼

Finally, observe that this definition of living consciously includes the practice of acting in accordance with one's knowledge. This point is essential. If I do not act on what I see and know, if my awareness is not reflected in my behavior—if my behavior *contradicts* my knowledge—I am in that regard not operating consciously. On the contrary, I am betraying consciousness. I evade what I know; I evade the motives for my evasion; I evade the fact that my behavior continues to defy my knowledge. Among other things, this is a sure formula for the undermining of self-esteem. It is also a sure formula for the undermining of one's long-term happiness and well-being. And yet people practice this betrayal every day, and when things go wrong, they wonder why life is so malevolent or why they are so "unlucky."

Thus: "I know I'm living beyond my means, but—; I know the way I eat is wrecking my health, but—; I know I ought to be giving more to my job and that I'm really unfair to my employer, but—; I know I ought to stop lying about my accomplishments, but—; I know it's wrong to abuse my children, but—; I know our policies are causing the business to go to hell, but—"

To some, "living consciously" may sound like an abstract idea. But in its consequences, it is as real as life and death.

WHAT MINDFULNESS ENTAILS AS A
WAY OF LIFE: AREAS TO BE CONSIDERED

In addressing this issue, I have broken it down into a number of categories. I have done so for purposes of discussion, but of course in reality they are all interdependent and interwoven.

We will examine what living consciously means with reference to

- taking pleasure in the functioning of our own mind
- our choices and actions
- seeking knowledge relevant to our goals and purposes
- avoidance impulses
- self-awareness
- relationships
- parenting
- the workplace
- the world—the context in which we live
- the realm of ideas, values, philosophy

THE JOY OF AWARENESS

In the opening of his *Metaphysics,* Aristotle declared that man by nature desires to know. It is possible he was paying the human race a compliment it did not entirely deserve. And yet, at the start of life we do exhibit pleasure in exploring the world with our senses, do struggle eagerly to find meaning in what we see and hear, do experience enjoyment in learning new things, do "desire to know." Later, encountering human irrationality, we may lose our fire, and awareness may become less appealing.

71

Or we may pass through an educational system that too often kills enthusiasm for thinking. Or our disowned problems and unhealed wounds may drive us to shrink consciousness self-defensively to a narrow band that leaves us cut off from the greater part of life. But all of us have experienced moments of exhilaration in the sheer act of seeing or hearing or understanding or grasping some new connection or driving ourselves to solve a difficult problem.

To the extent that one lives consciously, such moments are not rare exceptions or distant memories but reflect a central theme of one's existence.

In psychotherapy, I sometimes have the pleasure of awakening a client to this possibility. For example:

Hanna B. was a client with whom I did psychotherapy via the telephone some years ago. (Over fifty percent of my therapy practice is with clients who consult with me via the telephone from other cities.) Hanna was twenty-one years old, an art student, naturally intelligent but very unworldly, and, judging by a photograph she sent me, quite attractive. She was dating an "older man" of thirty-five who was the drama critic on one of the newspapers in the city where they lived. He had recently taken her to a series of parties following the season's leading theatrical events, and Hanna was mortified by her shyness, social anxiety, lack of sophistication, and inability to understand much of what people were saying. On the evening of the day we spoke, she was scheduled to attend the opening night's performance of a play, followed by a formal party where, she said, "everybody is going to be gorgeously dressed and have lots of clever things to say, and I'm going to be standing there like a dunce, and *what am I going to do?*"

I proposed that we conduct an experiment. I pointed out that one more social disappointment wouldn't really make that much difference, and there was a chance something unexpected might happen and something valuable might be learned if she would be willing to do what I suggested.

"From the moment you walk into the party," I said, "I'd like you to concentrate on noticing how much you can see and hear. Notice in detail what people are wearing. Notice the furniture and decorations in the room. Observe the color of the eyes of whoever you're talking to. Pay attention to the tone of voice in which people speak. Try to hear every word said in your presence. *Aggress on the environment with your senses."* We spent some time discussing how she would do this.

She telephoned next day to report, high with excitement. "It was quite amazing," she exclaimed. "First of all, I was so busy doing what you said and making sure I got it right that I had hardly any time to feel nervous. I kept thinking, 'Use your senses.' And also, putting all my focus outside myself, paying attention to my surroundings and the people, had an oddly calming effect. I felt stronger. I felt more like I was really there. Oh, this is so hard to explain. And then, the most wonderful thing of all was, when I paid attention, when I really listened to what people were saying, I discovered that it was pretty easy to understand them! I realized that I had been so sure it would all be over my head that I hadn't been listening on previous occasions, and so of course I couldn't understand, and that just strengthened my self-doubts. And here's the best part of all! I discovered that I had things to say, I had opinions! And when I expressed them, people listened to me! Oh God, what a night!"

"You've discovered the power of seeing and hearing," I answered.

Only then did I explain that when we are frightened, we typically pull energy *in* to our center, seeing less, hearing less—shrinking consciousness precisely when we need to *expand* it. The purpose of her assignment at the party was to keep her energy flowing *outward,* because if she did, consciousness would triumph over fear, as it did.

Further, I had a good deal of confidence in Hanna's intelligence, and I believed she had all the resources she needed to solve her problem once she was pointed in the right direction. However, if I had merely suggested that she bring a higher level of consciousness to that party, it is doubtful she (or anyone) would have known how to translate such a suggestion into action. By giving her something specific to do, something *actable* (to borrow a theater term), I hoped to stimulate a higher level of awareness and a new appreciation of her powers.

Later she said to me, "What I discovered was that I have a mind —and that *using it* is exciting."

This discovery was not the end of her journey but the beginning. It became the impetus for further learnings down the same road that would cultivate and strengthen her appreciation of her potentials. This is fairly typical. The most momentous leaps of growth commonly have as their springboard fairly modest first steps.

I do not wish to imply that I would use this same strategy with every client who presented a similar problem. But in this case, I knew Hanna quite well and suspected her level of development was such that nothing more ambitious would be needed to start her on her way. I might add that subsequent work in therapy was needed to solidify her new beginning and then extend and amplify it.

It need hardly be said that no one can force him- or herself to enjoy awareness, thinking, problem-solving, or any other worthwhile mental activity. Emotions cannot be commanded. And yet, having practiced psychotherapy for more than three decades, I have many memories of clients describing the pleasure they experienced in learning to live more consciously—not just reporting that their lives worked better or that their relationships were more satisfactory or that their careers progressed more successfully, but that sheer focused awareness itself felt more enjoyable. I stress this because of course there are people who do think but who associate thought with pain. (I recall a wonderful line in a short story by Ben Hecht I read in my twenties, in which Hecht speaks of people to whom thought comes with the impact of a toothache.) If consciousness is experienced as an onerous duty, one has not yet learned what it means to live consciously.

▲ ▲ ▲

When we are frightened, we typically pull energy *in* to our center, seeing less, hearing less—shrinking consciousness precisely when we need to *expand* it.

▼

Not uncommonly in psychotherapy (and everywhere else), one encounters men and women who resist awareness in some important aspects of life. Perhaps they are afraid to look at an unhappy marriage. Perhaps they are afraid to face the immorality of their behavior. Perhaps they do not want to look at the lies they live. Perhaps they do not want to look at how they treat their subordinates in the office. Perhaps they do not want to examine the anxious emptiness that rises within them whenever they are alone with nothing to do. Perhaps they do not want to examine a whole range of emotions they feel that clash with their official self-image. So they dread awareness, they dread quiet stillness, they dread meditative self-observation, they dread self-confrontation. They experience consciousness not as a source of pleasure but as a gun pointed at their head. That is because they identify "self" not with consciousness but with a phony image or with their favorite delusions.

They have never discovered that our "I"—our deepest identity—is neither our social roles nor our beliefs nor our feelings nor our attachments nor our defenses nor our possessions, but that inner searchlight we brighten or dim *by choice*.

When a person understands that who I am, ultimately and

essentially, is my faculty of awareness and my power to regulate its activity, the road is cleared to experience the joy of living mindfully. This joy can be manifest in the pleasure of contemplating the colors of sunlight flashing off a pebble, or the smell of clean air on a mountain hike, or the sounds of music, or the face of a loved one, or a favorite book to which one returns again and again, or one's own steps along the path of self-understanding, or the challenges of a difficult problem in business, mathematics, or philosophy.

In this state, the experience is: I = consciousness = aliveness.

▲ ▲ ▲

"I"—our deepest identity—is neither our social roles nor our beliefs nor our feelings nor our attachments nor our defenses nor our possessions, but that inner searchlight we brighten or dim *by choice.*

▼

CHOICES AND ACTIONS

One evening after giving a lecture, I went out with a group of people for coffee and conversation, and one man told me the following story: He had spent several hours trying unsuccessfully to correct some problem he was having with his automobile. He asked his five-year-old son to assist him by performing some task he thought was simple, but he did not explain clearly what he wanted and did not consider whether his request was realistic for a child.

When his son failed to do what was wanted, the father cried out in exasperation, "You can't do anything right!" The little boy stepped away from the car, and to the father's horror he overheard the boy muttering to himself, "You can't do anything right. You can't do anything right." The father dropped his tools, picked up his son, and begged his forgiveness, explaining that he had been upset and frustrated and did not mean what he had said.

"The things we are capable of saying," the father remarked to me sadly, "when we are not conscious of the words coming out of our mouths. That's why your observations tonight about living consciously struck me so forcefully."

▲ ▲ ▲

If we wish to *live* consciously, we need to be conscious of—and take responsibility for—the words coming out of our mouths.

▼

If we wish to parent consciously, we need to be aware of what we say to our children, remembering that what we say to them, they may later say to themselves—and in fact often do. Before we call a child stupid, sloppy, a coward, or bad, we need to ask ourselves: Do I really want my child to think of him- or herself in the terms I am about to use? Will that contribute to my child's healthy development? Will it foster growth and self-esteem? Does it serve my child's interests to learn self-contempt?

If we wish to *live* consciously, we need to be conscious of—and take responsibility for—the words coming out of our mouths.

And, of course, this principle applies to more than our relationships with children. It is quite common for husbands and wives who love each other to nonetheless say terrible things in the heat of an argument—things they will later regret, apologize for, and perhaps feel mortification at having said. Yet we know that words can wound. Long after a quarrel has seemingly been resolved, we remember the abusive, hurtful things said to us, and sometimes they fester in the soul for a very long time. Worse still, we may come to believe them—believe that we are "mean," "rotten," "stupid," "cowardly"—and then act accordingly. Insults that are internalized have the power to generate self-fulfilling prophecies.

So in the sphere of human relationships, it is a mark of high consciousness always to be aware of the issue: Am I willing to take responsibility for the words coming out of my mouth? Do I *intend* the reaction I am likely to evoke? (Recall the old and familiar definition of a gentleman: one who never insults anyone unintentionally.)

This conscientiousness is merely an instance of a wider issue: Am I conscious of and willing to take responsibility for my choices and actions?

▲ ▼ ▲

One of the ways we avoid taking responsibility for our actions when doing something we are not proud of or will be ashamed of later is *to blank out awareness in the moment of action that it is we who are doing what we are doing.*

We "find" ourselves striking our spouse. We "find" ourselves in bed with a stranger. We "find" we have emptied the bottle of scotch. We "find" we have broken our promise. We "find" we have spent on trivia the money we had been saving for an important need. We "find" we have been treating people with cruel lack of consideration. We "find" we have done nothing to correct our mistakes.

And too often, when we suffer the consequences of our unconsciousness, we do not ask, "How can I learn to be more conscious?" Instead we ask, "Why is life so difficult? Why do unhappy things always happen to me?"

To remain stuck in this predicament is humiliating. It is offensive to one's dignity. It deprives one of the experience of personal power. Today everyone is talking about self-esteem, and many people are saying they would like to learn how to cultivate it. Let the work begin here. There is no better beginning for self-esteem than a determination to choose and act consciously—and take responsibility.

▲ ▼ ▲

On a recent trip to Boston, I had lunch with a woman I had not seen in years. Elena is a writer, a management consultant, a wife, and a mother of four. After we had spent a while chatting, bringing each other up to date and getting reacquainted, I observed that she seemed sad, and I wondered aloud if there was some issue she was debating whether or not to raise.

Elena responded by saying that it was almost a decade since she had last written a book, that she badly missed writing, and that she was thinking about doing a new book. The problem, she explained, was that writing meant taking time away from her consulting practice, and with four children, she needed to supplement her husband's income with her own earnings. She could not know in advance what her book might do financially, and so she was torn between consulting and writing.

She then went on to itemize the enormous expense of raising four children in today's world, especially since all four were enrolled in private schools. The unspoken subtext of her words was: I love my children, but what a burden. I felt that in her eyes I saw the pain of watching her life unfold very differently than she had once imagined.

"Tell me," I asked gently and without reproach, "before you had your children, before you decided to have four—didn't you project what the cost would be and how your life would be affected?"

"To tell you the truth," she answered sadly, "I never thought about it."

This was a woman of high intelligence, but intelligence is no guarantee that anyone will always be as conscious as the situation requires. I did, however, go away from that lunch with the feeling that Elena had the resources to make the best realistic choices available to her, now that she seemed intent on bringing more awareness to the issues confronting her.

The tragedy of many lives is that we make the most fateful decisions with little or no awareness that our choices will change the shape and direction of our existence. This is one of the meanings of the idea that often people are sleepwalkers through the days and years of their time on earth. They make choices without conscious awareness of doing so. They commit themselves to actions without projecting the consequences. They are ruled more by impulse or routine or conformity to convention than by rational reflection.

This does not deny that their impulses may sometimes be good ones. Nor does it deny that their uncalculated actions may sometimes produce positive consequences. But as a basic way of life, their policy is dangerous. Choosing blindly is dangerous. Leaping without looking is dangerous. Living mechanically is dangerous. Letting others write one's life script is dangerous.

When people elect to operate without appropriate thought, they often profess astonishment at their unhappiness, as if the problem were that life is malevolent. "Why me?" they wonder, and of course the answer is, "Why not you, in light of your policies?" It is easy to seek escape from self-responsibility by retreating into a tragic sense of life.

"But it's so hard always to have to think about consequences," someone said to me when I related Elena's story in a lecture. "Sure, it's desirable to be aware. Who would argue with that? But don't you agree it's hard?"

"Not as hard as what she's going through now," I answered.

SEEKING KNOWLEDGE

Life consists of the pursuit of goals. These goals may be short-range or long-range, simple or complex, or anywhere in between: preparing a meal, acquiring the money for a new home, raising a child well, learning to meditate, developing a business, attaining an education, formulating a political philosophy, sculpting a figure, establishing a successful career, preparing one's organization for the challenges of the twenty-first century.

▲▲▲

Mindfulness leads to increased effectiveness; its abandonment leads to failure and defeat.

▼

To the extent we live consciously, we ask questions: If such is my goal, what do I need to do in order to achieve it? What information do I require? By what criteria will I judge whether I am on course or off course?

If, for example, I want to raise a happy, well-functioning child, how do I propose to do it? Is knowledge on this subject available that I should be studying? Are there relevant books I ought to be reading? What other useful resources exist? What do I need to know to do a good job? And what are the limits of what it is realistic to expect of myself? What is in my power and what isn't?

To the extent I operate consciously, I continually reach out for information relevant to my purposes. To the extent I don't, I assume knowledge is unnecessary, that I know all I need to know, or that what I don't know won't hurt me. So here the questions are: Do I stay alert to any information that might cause me to modify my course or correct my assumptions, or do I proceed on the premise that there is nothing new for me to learn? Do I continually seek out new data that might be helpful, or do I close my eyes even if it is presented? Mindfulness leads to increased effectiveness; its abandonment leads to failure and defeat.

▲ ▲ ▲

**If there is one certain indication of
unconscious living, it is indifference to the
question "What do I need to know (or learn)
in order to achieve my goals?"**

▼

During the last two decades, many companies lost market share or went out of existence entirely because leaders chose to ignore evidence that old ways of doing business were no longer appropriate—just as employees remain stuck and are passed over by colleagues because they choose to ignore evidence that they need to acquire new skills to remain adaptive in a rapidly changing economy—just as marriages break down because one or both partners choose to ignore evidence that their behavior is destroying the relationship—just as children grow up without learning self-responsibility or self-discipline because parents believe all they have to do is feel "love" and that no knowledge or skill is needed to raise a human being properly.[1]

If there is one certain indication of unconscious living, it is indifference to the question "What do I need to know (or learn) in order to achieve my goals?" Such indifference is intimately related to the absence of a sense of reality. When that sense is lacking, when there is little or no grasp of facts or objectivity, goals (it is imagined) are achieved by wishing, not by appropriate action.

A relationship of reciprocal causation exists between the practice of living consciously and self-esteem. Just as living consciously strengthens self-esteem, so self-esteem inspires living consciously. If we have confidence in our mind, we are not deterred by the challenges of new learning. Persevering, we tend to succeed in our efforts, which reinforces our initial confidence. Lacking such confidence, the challenges of new learning may feel intimidating and overwhelming—change and novelty tend to be perceived as frightening—and so one tends to cling to the known and familiar. But if the known and familiar are inadequate to the requirements of the new situation, the result is failure and the deterioration of an already wounded self-esteem.

When the self-fulfilling prophecy is a positive one, our expectations work on our behalf. When it is negative, they work against us. In the latter instance, the challenge is to break out of the vicious circle, to interrupt the pattern of self-sabotage.

In therapy, I often find it useful to give a client the sentence stem "If I brought five percent more consciousness to my work—" When, through sentence completion, the client identifies the more productive behaviors that would follow a raising of consciousness, I coach him or her to practice those behaviors. The result is that consciousness expands, work progresses more satisfactorily, self-esteem rises, and a negative pattern is interrupted.

Tony L. was a twenty-nine-year-old real estate broker who entered the profession shortly before the real estate market in southern California went into major decline. Consequently, Tony was experiencing great difficulty in earning a living. He was not too self-confident to begin with, was prone to feel defeated in the face of any obstacle, and now his situation seemed close to hopeless.

But when I asked if anyone in his office was doing well in spite of the tough market, he remarked that there was one older woman —Miriam—whose sales remained consistently high. I wondered aloud what Miriam might know that others in her office seemed not to know.

When Tony was working with the sentence completion "If I brought five percent more consciousness to my work—," one of his endings was: "I would learn from Miriam what she does that's different from what I do."

It took several weeks of working on his self-concept, his passivity, and his insecurities before he was ready to approach Miriam and ask for her help.

Fortunately, she agreed to be his mentor. She talked at length about how she acquired listings of new properties, how she made her presentations to potential buyers, and what she did to make it as easy as possible for customers to buy her offerings. I worked with him on lists of specific questions to ask her. She agreed to have him accompany her on some appointments so he could observe first-hand how she worked. I had him write a paper on everything he was learning, entitled "Miriam's Sales Secrets."

While my immediate goal was to assist Tony in becoming a better salesman, I had a deeper agenda: to facilitate his discovering that he was capable of learning anything he needed to learn to advance his life. Or, to say it a bit differently, my deeper agenda was to strengthen his self-esteem so as to better equip him for any life challenge and not merely the immediate one of a troublesome real estate market.

Since I wanted him to confront the ways in which he sabotaged himself, I gave him the sentence stem "One of the ways I contribute to my own frustration is—" He articulated such endings as "I just sit and feel sorry for myself; I tell myself I'm stupid and worthless; I daydream too much; I joke and put myself down when with clients; I act flaky; I don't project that I'm a serious person; sometimes I come on too hungry and desperate."

Another sentence stem that proved helpful was "One of the hard things about translating what I'm learning into action is—" His endings included "I'd have to change; I'd have to put myself out there; I'd have to risk failing; Father always told me I was a loser; I don't see myself as successful; I'd have to get off of feeling self-pity; I'd have to be self-responsible; I'd have to think more; I might become someone I don't know."

Whereas previously he had been focusing only on external obstacles, our work led him to focus on internal obstacles. He became more conscious of the forces within that had to be dealt with if he were to break free. (One of the reasons sales training programs sometimes fail to produce desired results is that they do not address the self-concept of the students that may contain any number of limiting beliefs.)

As we worked through his fears and confronted these limiting beliefs, he gathered the courage to experiment with the tactics he had learned from his office mentor, and his sales record slowly began to climb. But then an interesting and unanticipated development took place. He announced that he wanted to look for a "more interesting and intellectually stimulating" way to earn a living. At first I wondered if this was a new form of self-sabotage, but I became convinced that, to the contrary, it was a sign of genuine growth.

He explained, "I stupidly thought that real estate was a good line to get into because it didn't require much in terms of intelligence. Now I not only know how wrong I was, but more importantly, I know that I don't have to hold myself down to something I think is easy. Not that real estate turned out to be so easy. But if I can learn this, I can learn something else that might be more exciting for me. I don't know where I'll end up, but—the sky's the limit. I mean, why shouldn't I find out what I've got inside me?"

This is not a discussion of psychotherapy, and my story omits a great deal. I am isolating only those elements that bear on the issue we are examining here. This is true of all the therapy vignettes in this book.

Just as living consciously entails taking responsibility for learning what is needed to achieve our goals, so it entails knowing where we are, relative to our goals at any time.

If one of my goals is to have a satisfying marriage, what is the present state of my marriage? Do I know? Would my partner and I answer the same way? Are we happy with each other? Are there frustrations and unresolved issues? If so, what am I doing about them?

If one of my goals is to build my business and increase my market share, what am I doing about it? Am I closer to the goal than I was a year ago? What are the signs that I am on track or off? What are my criteria for measuring progress?

If one of my goals is to earn my living as an artist, where am I at present relative to this aspiration? Am I any closer than I was a year ago? Do I have grounds for believing I will be closer next year? By what standards do I judge?

▲ ▲ ▲

**Living consciously entails paying attention to
the relationship between our professed values,
goals, and purposes and our daily behavior.**

▼

Think of some long- or medium-term goal of your own. Ask yourself where you stand in relation to it, as compared with a year ago. Are you making progress? What are the indicators?

"For ten years," a client said to me, "I've dreamed of getting out of technical writing for engineering manuals and writing a novel instead. And for most of those ten years, I did absolutely nothing about it—except tell myself, 'Someday.' Then you asked what I would be doing if I converted my dream into a conscious purpose. That was the question to ask. I felt like someone shot cold water on me out of a fire hose—when I was sound asleep. Talk about instant enlightenment. Here's my updated report: I've got a thirty-page outline of the story plus the first three chapters written. And now I'm looking for a literary agent. But the depressing thought is—I might have gone on sleeping for who knows how much longer. 'Thou shalt be conscious'—that should be the first commandment."

▲ ▼ ▲

Living consciously entails paying attention to the relationship between our professed values, goals, and purposes and our daily behavior. Sometimes there is lack of congruence between what we say our priorities are and how we invest our time and energy. We may give least attention to that which we profess to value most while giving most of our attention to what we say is of lesser importance. In business organizations we encounter this problem all the time, when executives invest time and energy in less productive activities at the expense of those activities that would best serve the organization's mission. The same problem shows up in our personal lives—when, for instance, we spend a great deal of time with people who are not that important to us while depriving the members of our family, whom we profess to love more than anyone else in the world, of our attention and companionship. So if we are mindful, we monitor our actions relative to our goals. We seek to know where there is alignment and where there is misalignment. If there is misalignment, we recognize that either our actions or our goals need to be rethought.

Notice I do not take it as self-evident that it is our actions which must change. True, more often than not it is our actions which we elect to modify, but that should not be taken as a foregone conclusion. Sometimes our actions reflect a subconscious wisdom superior to our conscious, official commitment. We may have adopted goals that do not represent our deepest values or serve our true interests, which is why at some level we are pulled in another direction. I once signed a contract to write a book on a particular subject but found that in the writing I kept giving space to another subject entirely, until I realized that the latter was the book I really needed to write at that time in my life. So the contract was revised in favor of the subject that was more important to me. I revised my original goal—and wrote *The Six Pillars of Self-Esteem*. A discrepancy between our goals and our actions is a signal that increased awareness is needed in this area, but it does not say what the outcome of our new thinking will be.

▲▲▲

Doing more of what doesn't work doesn't work.

▼

In pursuing our values and goals mindfully, we pay attention not only to our actions but also to their outcome. Are our actions producing the results we anticipated? Our actions may be perfectly in alignment with our values, goals, and purposes, but the problem is that we miscalculated what our actions would achieve. If we are operating mechanically, it is very easy to be oblivious to this fact and go on repeating what does not work without ever drawing nearer our destination.

So we need feedback from the environment to be able to adjust or correct our course when necessary. To be open to such feedback is one of the meanings of being mindful—paying attention—living consciously.

The principle of paying attention to outcome has contributed enormously to my growth as a psychotherapist. I may hear a client's problem and believe I know the process by which we will solve it. But suppose that in spite of our best efforts, the problem persists. At this point, I realize there is something I have failed to discover or factor into the treatment, and the result is that I am ineffective. In seeking to learn what it would take to succeed, I may be led to a new understanding of the problem or a new treatment strategy, or both. Noticing what doesn't work is for many therapists the launching pad to new discoveries—when the therapist is in a mindful state. The mistake not to make, however, is stubbornly to persist in what is not working and/or blame the client's "recalcitrance"—because there is no learning in such a policy.

As someone has observed, doing more of what doesn't work doesn't work. If we are operating a business and our ads are performing calamitously below expectations, we may need to rethink the content of the ads, the media in which we advertise, our assessment of the market, or even our offering itself. What we do not do is ritualistically keep running the same ad. If our child's behavior is unacceptable to us and our sole response is to give lectures and make threats and the behavior does not change, the solution is not to give longer lectures or make louder threats. The solution is to discover an alternative way of responding that yields better results. This requires that we bring a higher level of consciousness to the situation. If we are a legislator who sponsors programs that not only fail to solve the problem addressed but result in a worsening of that problem, the solution is not to spend more money or pass more laws. The solution is to reexamine our premises. However, when programs are paid for out of the public treasury, there is no great incentive to pay attention to outcome or to painstakingly rethink our assumptions. When there is little accountability, there is little felt need to raise the level of our consciousness.

If we are emotionally invested in a given position, role, practice, or belief, it may be difficult to challenge and rethink it, in spite of evidence that it leads to undesirable results—results that may be the opposite of our intention. It is often easier to rationalize failure, make scapegoats of innocent parties, or demand more money and wider powers to make our program work. We may experience it as a blow to our self-esteem (as well as, sometimes, our vested interests) to confront what our ideas and actions lead to in reality.

If, however, we are wise enough to base our self-esteem not on being "right" but on being rational—on being conscious—and on having integrity, then we recognize that acknowledgment and correction of an error is not an abyss into which we have fallen but a height we can take pride in having climbed.

This leads us to another aspect of living consciously: awareness of our avoidance impulses and determination to manage them rather than be ruled by them.

▲ ▲ ▲

If we are wise enough to base our self-esteem not on being "right" but on being rational— on being conscious—and on having integrity, then we recognize that acknowledgment and correction of an error is not an abyss into which we have fallen but a height we can take pride in having climbed.

▼

MANAGING AVOIDANCE IMPULSES

Nothing is intrinsically irrational about the impulse to pull back from that which is frightening or painful. All of us have such impulses. But if we have a well-developed sense of reality—and a capacity for self-discipline—we recognize that there are circumstances in which it is dangerous to allow fear and pain to have the last word. Sometimes we need to do things that scare us. Sometimes we need to look at things that are painful. If we don't, the consequences will be bad for us. Understanding this, we know that sometimes all we can do is draw a deep breath and proceed.

I have already given many examples of issues we may not wish to face; further examples are unnecessary. The point I wish to make here is that one application of mindfulness is that of learning to *manage* the feeling that pulls us away from where we need to look. We can witness the feeling without succumbing to it. We can give the last word to judgment rather than impulse. This is a discipline that must be learned, and it would be foolish to suggest it is always easy—it is not. The first step is to grasp that such a possibility exists. The next is to make reaching such a goal a conscious purpose and not merely a wish or desire or "intention."

I can be aware of the great fear I feel about fully confronting the rage I feel toward a parent, the sexual attraction I feel toward a sibling, the satisfaction I feel in my spouse's suffering, or the humiliation I felt at the hands of my classmates as a child. I can experience a powerful impulse to blank out such awareness. And still, I can gently pull my mind back to where it needs to look, I can will myself to stand in the presence of that which I need to understand—I can choose to remain conscious. I can rule rather than be ruled by my avoidance impulses. I can value growth above immediate comfort.

▲ ▲ ▲

**One application of mindfulness is that of
learning to *manage* the feeling that pulls us
away from where we need to look.**

▼

To many people, the thought never occurs that they have a choice. They imagine that if they feel fear or pain, this is the end of it—there is nothing further to think about. Any experience of discomfort is interpreted as a stop sign, not to be questioned or challenged. It may be a revelation for them to discover that this need not be the case, that they can feel the fear or pain and proceed nonetheless.

No one accomplishes this practice with perfect consistency. Sometimes the seductive pull of unconsciousness wins. Self-esteem asks not for flawless consistency but for the earnest *determination* to be as conscious as one can be, to manage awareness to the best of one's ability—which does require self-discipline and self-responsibility.

A simple sentence-completion exercise that is usually helpful in this context (done daily for at least a week) consists of writing six to ten endings for the stem "If I bring five percent more consciousness to my fear (anxiety, pain, sadness, anger, this situation, this problem, or whatever)—" Radiating the dreaded area with awareness tends (if not instantly, then eventually) to reduce discomfort and generate deeper levels of understanding of what needs to be solved or healed.

Indeed, new light can be cast on almost any problem one has been avoiding by doing the exercise "If I bring five percent more consciousness to X—" (where "X" is the problem).

Thus: If I bring five percent more consciousness to

- my emotions—
- my needs—
- my deepest longings—
- my deepest frustrations—
- my anxiety—
- my depression—
- my relationship with my mother (or father)—
- my relationship with my spouse (or child, or boss, or subordinate, or colleague, or friend)—
- my fear of self-assertiveness—
- my passivity—
- my procrastination—

And then one writes endings as rapidly and freely as one can, allowing the unfamiliar and unexpected to emerge, stimulating the mind toward new understandings and new integrations and, ultimately, to the kinds of mind shifts that result in new behaviors.

As I said earlier, to do the exercise effectively, one must let go of censorship or withholding or trying to be "deep" or "meaningful" and be willing to turn out endings, any endings, as spontaneously as possible. If one gets stuck for an ending, *invent*. The freedom to write *anything* becomes sooner or later the freedom to write something important. I find this tool invaluable in the practice of psychotherapy, but there is no reason a person cannot learn and experiment with it on his or her own.[2]

SELF-AWARENESS

Observe that the subject of self-awareness keeps coming up in every issue we discuss. Learning to recognize our avoidance impulses and not be controlled by them is only one instance. Another is learning to recognize our self-sabotaging patterns—ways we subvert our own growth and ambitions and keep ourselves stuck precisely where we claim we do not wish to be. A favorite exercise of mine when working with social relations consists of giving a client the sentence stem "One of things I want from people and don't know how to get is—" followed by "One of the ways I make it difficult for people to give me what I want is—" followed by "One of the ways I contribute to my own frustration is—" followed by "If any of what I'm saying is true—" A typical series of responses might be as follows:

One of the things I want from people and don't know how to get is—

respect
concern for my feelings
help
interest in my needs
friendship
good conversation
love

kindness
cooperation
interest in spending time with me

One of the ways I make it difficult for people to give me what I want is—

I act like I don't want anything.
I don't tell them what I want.
I act indifferent.
I withdraw.
I project that I'm totally self-sufficient.
I'm cold and distant.
I give and give and give and make of my giving a wall no one can
    get through.
I'm inaccessible.

One of the ways I contribute to my own frustration is—

I reject people before they can reject me.
I send out mixed and confusing signals.
I surrender to fear of being hurt.
I act like I don't care.
I don't give people a chance.
When people try to give to me, I convey nothing they do is right.
I don't reach out, and then I just feel sorry for myself.

If any of what I'm saying is true—

I have to be more open.
I have to put myself out there.
I have to give people a chance.

I have to let them see me.

I have to stop hiding my needs and wants.

I have to be willing to ask.

I have to bring more benevolence to my relationships.

I have to drop my image.

I have to show my vulnerability and not be ashamed of it.

As we become aware of what we do that does not serve our interests, the option arises of choosing to act differently. We may or may not exercise that option. So yet another application of self-awareness is observing what our mental processes are and how we subsequently act when confronted by the fact that our characteristic behavior in some context is inappropriate and counterproductive. Do we look—or look away? Do we seek a better alternative—or mechanically repeat what we already know is a mistake?

These remarks are offered as only the briefest introduction to the subject of self-awareness and its relation to living consciously. We will return to this in chapters 4 and 5. We will see that self-awareness includes consciousness of our mental processes, our values, our emotions, and our actions, and that *self-alienation*—a condition of estrangement from and unconsciousness of such matters—is a prime cause of suffering and ineffectiveness.

But first, let us complete our review of the basics of what a conscious life looks like.

4

A Conscious Life—2: Bringing to Our Pursuits the Awareness They Require

TWO broad areas in which the issue of living consciously arises for all of us are relationships and work. When we deal with another human being, we can bring a greater or lesser level of consciousness to the encounter. When we confront the tasks of the day, we can do so mindfully or we can bring minimal attention and thought. In both cases, we have choices and are responsible for the level of awareness we generate.

We do not live and work in a vacuum. We exist in a physical and social world; we are participants in a culture. We may be more or less aware of the ways we are affected by the wider world that constitutes our environment. Some people are utterly oblivious to the influences that affect them; others are keenly sensitive. We may bring more or less consciousness to the wider context in which we live and act.

All of us are moved by ideas and values of which we may or may not be consciously aware. We hold premises, implicit if not explicit, about the nature of man and woman, the things that most matter in life, the ways human beings should relate to one another, right and wrong, good and evil, the meaning of work, love, and sex, the nature of justice, the relationship of the individual to society and the government, and so on. When asked to articulate their beliefs, people often have difficulty. Their philosophy is largely subconscious and has never been brought into the light of full awareness. This makes it more difficult to check against reality or to revise; they are stuck with old thinking that might not even have been theirs in the first place but merely absorbed uncritically from others.

These are the matters we will examine in this chapter.

CONSCIOUS RELATIONSHIPS

▲ ▲ ▲

One of the ways we convey respect for another human being is through the consciousness we bring to the encounter—that is, through seeing, hearing, and responding in a way that allows the other individual to feel understood.

▼

The level of consciousness we bring to another person is often a function of the nature of the relationship. We ordinarily do not bring the same level of attention to the waiter who takes our dinner order as we bring to the person with whom we are having dinner. We bring the level needed, presumably, for basic courtesy, but no more than that, unless we are in a very sociable mood or unless something about the waiter sparked our interest. (Some people—whom we call rude—do not bring even the basic minimum.) Rationally, the more important the relationship is to us, the more intense the level of awareness we bring to it and the deeper our mind seeks to penetrate. Thus, if we love consciously (in contrast to being blindly infatuated), we almost certainly understand that person better than we understand anyone else.

On any level of intimacy, one of the ways we convey respect for another human being is through the consciousness we bring to the encounter—that is, through seeing, hearing, and responding in a way that allows the other individual to feel understood. And one of the ways disrespect is conveyed is through lack of consciousness, as when our inattentive behavior implies: Who you are and what you think and feel are not worthy of my attention. Not uncommonly, people of high position and low self-esteem flaunt their power by dismissing others with this latter signal. At minimum, consciousness is the beginning of civility in human relationships.

I have written, at length, elsewhere about our need for psychological visibility, by which I mean our need to experience being perceived and responded to appropriately by other human beings.[1] We have a deep-rooted need to be seen, understood, and appreciated in ways congruent with our self-perceptions. It is thus that we are enabled to experience a form of *objectivity* about our self and its expressions—therefore a form of self-affirmation.

The need for this experience is inherent in our nature, and when it is frustrated, growth and overall well-being may be adversely affected. When children are treated not as persons but as annoying objects or lovable playthings, they feel invisible—unseen by and unreal to adults—and self-esteem is a frequent casualty. If a man experiences being seen by his wife not as a human being but as a success object[2] or a performance machine—or when a wife experiences being seen by her husband not as a person but as a sex object or a trophy—again, a sense of invisibility results, and the relationship suffers accordingly. The wordless cry "When you deal with me, please *see* me" means "When you deal with me, please be conscious." (And, to say it once more, "please be conscious" means "please be *appropriately* conscious.")

When we bring a high level of consciousness to an encounter with another, we are conscious, on the one hand, of what the person is saying, how the person is looking, and the subtler emotional undertone of his or her communications. We register more information than the literal content of the words spoken. And on the other hand, we are conscious of our own words and our own emotional undertone and the multiple signals we ourselves are sending (at least to some extent). We are naïve if we imagine that all the other person receives or reacts to are our verbal statements. So if we are operating mindfully, we recognize the complexities of our exchanges, and to varying degrees our responses reflect our awareness.

Not all encounters require this high level of awareness. As already noted, context determines what constitutes an appropriate level of consciousness. But let us consider: what does it mean to operate consciously in romantic love?

To love another human being is to know and love his or her person. This presupposes a commitment to seeing and understanding the object of our love. "Love" without sight or knowledge is a contradiction in terms. What would it mean to say "I love you" if I neither see you nor know who you are nor exhibit any desire to do so? It can only mean "Please don't distract me with the reality of who you are. I am preoccupied with my dream of you."

Many people have an affair with or marry not a person but a fantasy—then resent the person for not being like their fantasy and then withdraw in bitterness, telling themselves, "So much for romantic love." They do not examine the mental processes that led to their selection of a partner; instead, they are angry at a universe in which the road of unconsciousness does not lead to fulfillment.

The reasons why we fall in love with someone are admittedly complex; not all of them are readily accessible to explicit awareness. One of the pleasures of lovers is seeking to identify on deeper and deeper levels the traits that inspire and excite them in their partner. This process can go on for years and can be a continuing source of pleasure and increasing intimacy.

However, from early in the relationship, we can begin to reflect: What is it about this person that most stimulates and attracts me? What factors are psychological or spiritual and which are physical? What do I like about what this person projects? What do I see in this person's character that I admire? Do I have any reservations or misgivings? If so, what do they concern, and how can I check them out? What do I dislike (if anything), and what importance does that have for me in the scale of my values? What do we seem to have in common, and why do I think so? In what ways might we be incompatible, and why do I think so?

We may not be able—ever—to name *all* the elements that inspire our love and attraction, but that should not stop us from seeking to identify as much as we can, because that is one of the ways love and intimacy deepen, assuming that the relationship is basically solid and healthy.

Working with couples, I often give them an exercise where they sit opposite one other and take turns doing spoken sentence completions (to one other) for such stems as "One of the things I appreciate about you is—" followed by "One of things I'd like you to know about me is—" Such exercises facilitate the exchange of visibility.

A man who felt quite invisible to his wife asked her one day, "What do you love about me?" She was unable to answer. It became apparent that her love affair wasn't with him but with a highly subjective *idea* of him in her mind (the man she *needed* him to be). When challenged by the actual man in the real world, she became tongue-tied and helpless. She may have loved him in some way of her own, but it was not a conscious love or a love that could inspire in him the experience of being seen and understood.

We cannot be conscious of another in the way I am suggesting if we are not also reasonably self-aware. One of the ways I know you is by observing the ways you affect me. One of the ways I discover who you are is by identifying the way I experience myself in our interactions. If I do not know my own values, I am unlikely to be able to articulate what I value in you. If we are strangers to ourselves, others will be strangers to us.

Included in self-awareness is awareness of personal factors that can distort our perception. It is easy enough for loneliness or need to distort the thinking of a fairly rational person; if we at least recognize our state, we can better arm ourselves against the kind of wishful thinking that can lead us into a noxious relationship. A woman who had been badly hurt in a disastrous love affair said,

"After Jack, I know how vulnerable I am now. Someone who treated me decently—showed real kindness—could probably have me imagining I was in love when I wasn't."

A psychologist of my acquaintance angrily rejected this entire line of thought. "Romantic love *requires* blindness," he insisted. "Passion dies in the light."

"Do you mean," I answered, "that no one who really understood you could possibly be in love with you? Maybe so. But why lay that charge against the whole human race?"

In contrast, a happily married woman I know once said to me, "If we're willing to look without blinders, if we're willing to see everything that's there to be seen, shortcomings as well as strengths —and if we still love passionately—that's what I call mature, romantic love."[3]

▲ ▼ ▲

When we enter a love relationship, we do so with certain implicit or explicit wants and expectations. Do we know what ours are? Do we know what our partner's are? Do we feel a responsibility to give that which we would like to receive (or its equivalent)? If we love mindfully, the answers will be in the affirmative.

But of course, many people do not love mindfully. I am thinking of men and women who are very clear about the fact that if anything is troubling them, they want and expect their partner to be fully available to them, fully interested in what they have to say, unreservedly present and compassionate. They are oblivious to the fact that their partner desires the same of them, and oblivious also to how rarely they give it. Psychologically, they have never evolved beyond the pattern of a child-parent relationship, which is essentially unequal: one person does most or all of the taking; the other does most or all of the giving.

Each one of us has a responsibility in a relationship for knowing what we are receiving and what we are giving. We need to know how we feel about the quality of the exchange and also how our partner feels. One of the surest indicators of trouble is when one partner feels he or she is giving much more than he or she is receiving. (Studies suggest that this is also the situation in which infidelity is most likely; the partner who is giving more feels "entitled." The problem of infidelity is relatively less likely to arise when partners feel their contribution is equal.) As to knowing how our partner feels about the exchange, usually the simplest way to find out is to ask—and be willing to listen undefensively, with an interest in learning rather than in justifying our own behavior. Defensiveness is the enemy of consciousness.

▲ ▼ ▲

Each of us brings into a relationship certain assets and certain shortcomings. Do we know what they are? What do we bring to a relationship that our partner is likely to find valuable? What do we bring that a partner may find difficult or troublesome?

When a couple consults me because of problems in their relationship, I often ask each of them to tell me what might be hard about being married to him or her. If they have some insight on this matter, it is more hopeful than if they find the question incomprehensible or unanswerable. A wife said to me, "Difficult about being married to me? I can't imagine. I'm a good cook, I never deny Harry sex, I'm an excellent hostess, and I'm told I'm attractive. What does Harry want? He keeps saying there's more to life than work and entertaining. Well, like what? I wish he'd tell me. But some people are never satisfied. If only you can get Harry to see that really his life is quite happy." Sometimes a partner pretends to be conscientiously naming a shortcoming, but it is only a disingenuous self-compliment, as when a husband said to me, "I'm very reasonable and fair-minded. It's one of my faults, I suppose. I think at times Jenny finds it intimidating."

Often I have partners face each other and do sentence-completion exercises using such stems as "One of the ways I can be difficult is—" followed by "Sometimes I can be frustrating when I—" followed by "Sometimes I make you angry when—" followed by "Sometimes I hurt you when—" followed by "One of the things you want from me and don't always get is—"

When people get into the swing of the process, it is remarkable how much they realize they know at a subconscious level and how much they are able to make conscious and articulate once they make a commitment to the sentence-completion path.

The example given above deals with negatives. On the positive side, consciousness is also raised by stems such as "One of the things we enjoy about each other is—" followed by "One of the things we have in common is—" followed by "I appreciate it when you—" followed by "I feel especially loved when you—" followed by "I feel most connected with you when—"

Occasionally, not often, this exercise breaks down when a couple is brought face-to-face with the fact that they have little or nothing positive to say and that their relationship is essentially empty of values. If this fact is confronted rather than denied, this, too, is a victory of consciousness, even though a result may be the decision to go their separate ways.

However, the far more common reaction to this exercise is that the couple is reconnected to that which inspired them to fall in love in the first place. It is consciousness that keeps love alive. It is unconsciousness that drives the transition from love to boredom to emotional deadness.

▲ ▲ ▲

**If we love consciously, we are aware that how
we respond to our partner entails a continuing
process of choice.**

▼

Talk to people who have remained deeply in love over many years and you will find that they operate at a high level of mindfulness with regard to their partners. They do not take their partners for granted. They remain conscious of the values and traits that initially inspired their love, and they note those values and traits in their daily encounters and interactions. They have retained the capacity to see and to appreciate. Their love is *mentally active.*

If people are mentally passive, *no* excitement can last, neither romantic love nor any other passion.

And if mental passivity is taken as *normal* and active awareness as *abnormal,* then the idea of enduring love can only be perceived as a delusion, and *ennui* as our natural condition.

▲▼▲

If we love consciously, we are aware that how we respond to our partner entails a continuing process of choice. If my partner expresses a wish or desire, I am conscious of how I respond and conscious that I am making a choice. If my partner conveys a need or a desire, whatever I elect to do about it is done consciously. Further, I do not take my mood of the moment as the ultimate authority nor the infallible guide as to how I am to act. Loving consciously entails sometimes doing things we are not in the mood to do. Not just love but *all* my values require it. (Am I in the "mood" to work every day when I sit down at my computer? Clearly not. But I do it—and do not regard the act as self-sacrifice.) Sometimes, with the best will in the world I am unable to do what my partner wishes, but this does not prevent me from treating those wishes with respect. I can communicate caring even in situations where I cannot accommodate.

▲▼▲

There are great differences among people in the level of consciousness they typically bring to their romantic relationships. Some people, a minority, operate at a very high level. Many more tolerate a truly astonishing level of unawareness regarding what they claim is the most important relationship of their life. Home, they seem to feel, is where they get to rest from the burden of consciousness that life in the workplace imposes on them.

Loving consciously does not mean subjecting one's relationship to endless "analysis." Often such "analysis" is an exercise that has very little, if anything, to do with being more conscious. Rather, I am speaking of simple seeing and hearing. Paying attention. Giv-

ing feedback. Noticing one's own feelings and those of one's partner. Noticing the nature of the interactions with one's partner.
Noticing expressions of warmth and caring or the lack thereof.
Noticing the character of the relationship as it is created anew
each day.

One of the most significant things to notice is how conflict is
handled. When friction erupts, who does what? Is the focus on
finding a solution or finding fault, on understanding or blaming
(or defending)? Are differences approached in a spirit of benevolence or one of fear and hostility? What has priority—protecting
the relationship or self-justification? If estrangement sets in, who
typically makes the first move to overcome it? What is the other
partner doing in the meantime?

If we don't like what we see, we have the option of experiment-
ing with different behaviors. But that option doesn't fully come
into existence until we face what our behavior is now. If the root
of all evil is the act of dismissing reality, the root of all virtue is
respect for reality.

*How consciously are you operating as you read these words? Are you
thinking about what they mean in terms of your own life? Or is the
whole discussion floating in the realm of remote (and safe) abstraction?*

Here again, we can observe the reciprocal relationship between
self-esteem and operating consciously. The higher our self-esteem,
the more likely we are to operate consciously (and benevolently)
in our relationship. The more we operate consciously (and benevolently), the more we nourish our self-esteem. And of course, the
reverse is also true. This is one of the reasons why a relationship
can be a vehicle for personal growth. Through learning to meet
its challenges, one evolves as a person.

CONSCIOUS PARENTING

I discuss many aspects of effective parenting in *The Six Pillars of
Self-Esteem,* and above I commented on the importance of being
aware of the messages one's words convey to a child, but here I
want to offer a few additional observations.

To parent consciously is, first of all, to think through the responsibilities entailed by choosing to bring a child into the world. Physical caretaking is only the most obvious necessity. Beyond that is the more challenging task of preparing a child for independent survival as an adult.

That need is filled in part, but only in part, by providing a child with an adequate education, whereby he or she can acquire the knowledge and skills to earn a living in the marketplace. It is the parents' job to inspire in the child an understanding of the importance of being able to support and take care of oneself—the value of independence—and this is as much an imperative for girls as for boys.

Unfortunately, parents often send very different signals to their sons and daughters, stressing achievement goals far more for boys than for girls. Parents therefore need to ask themselves, Do I want my daughter to regard dependency as her natural state? Do I want her to be imprisoned in an unhappy marriage one day because she feels inadequate to the challenges of the marketplace? Or do I want her to face life with self-assurance and a sense of basic competence?

Indeed, this leads us to a wider set of questions parents need to address, all of which bear on parenting consciously:

What, fundamentally, do I want for my child? For instance, do I want my child to have self-esteem? If so, what do I see as my contribution to that result—and why do I think so? Or do I wish my child to have a negative self-concept—and how do I think that will affect his or her behavior?

Do I want my child to think critically and independently? Or am I content to have my child leave thinking to other people and go along with whatever they decide? And if it is the former I desire, how do I plan to inspire that practice? (There are, for example, parents who make a point of watching television shows with their children, including commercials, and teaching them how to spot flawed logic, misleading implications, implicit value messages—and encouraging their children to examine what they see and hear *consciously*. "This story conveys that it's 'cool' and even admirable to get the things one wants by lies and violence. What's your opinion about that?" "This show suggests that there's something charming and even hilarious about driving an automobile while high on drugs. How does that strike you?" "Did the advertising for that product make sense to you?" "Did you understand what that politician was saying? Did it seem consistent with what we heard him say in that interview last week? Or do you think he contradicted himself?")

Do I want my child to deal with others honestly, fairly, and benevolently? How do I teach that? Or do I want my child always to look for the short-term advantage, regardless of honesty or fairness—and why?

Do I want my child to learn appropriate self-assertiveness and to respect his or her legitimate interests in interactions with others? How will I teach that? Or do I want my child to practice self-sacrifice and self-denial, always placing others above self—and why is that my preference? And if my child asks why everyone else's wants must always be treated as more important, how will I answer?

Do I want my child to be self-accepting and self-compassionate—or self-critical and self-condemning? Why? And how do I propose to encourage the result I want? Will I convey the acceptance and compassion I want my child to internalize?

Do I want my child to acquire a rational set of values? If so, what do I think are rational values—and why do I think so? And how will I convey them? Do I exemplify what I want to teach? Do I see myself as an appropriate model of moral behavior? If not, if my child sees a discrepancy between what I teach and what I practice, what do I imagine he or she will conclude? Do I want that? If not, what am I prepared to do about it?

▲ ▲ ▲

**Parenting consciously asks a high level of
clarity and honesty in examining one's own
desires and resolving conflicts among them, or**

**at least doing one's best not to send conflicting
signals.**

▼

Often, parents are confused about what they want. For example, they may want their children to think independently when it comes to considering the opinions of other people but to accept unreservedly, on "faith," whatever ideas the parents convey. A mother may want her daughter to have a successful marriage but not one conspicuously happier than her own. A father may want his son to do well in his career but not make conspicuously more money than the father. So parenting consciously asks a high level of clarity and honesty in examining one's own desires and resolving conflicts among them, or at least doing one's best not to send conflicting signals.

While most parents are aware of the financial responsibilities involved in raising children—or, at any rate, are forced to confront them eventually—there is rarely a corresponding awareness of the intellectual responsibilities demanded. If they vaguely grasp that a great deal of thinking is involved, they tend not to focus on that fact—to dismiss it from consciousness and to tell themselves that they will "just know" what to do. Perhaps they tell themselves that for millions of years people have been raising children without going through all that much thinking. True enough, they have. But the results of that policy are what cry out that a better way needs to be found—that the costs of unconsciousness in terms of suffering have been staggering.

The first step toward conscious parenting consists not of answering the questions listed above, which will not always be easy, but of asking them—and of staying connected to their importance.

CONSCIOUSNESS IN THE WORKPLACE

When working with clients on career issues or consulting with executives in business organizations, I often have them begin by writing or verbalizing endings for the sentence stem "If I bring five percent more consciousness to my work—" In this way, three points are established immediately:

that we have options about the degree of consciousness we bring to our work;

that it is possible to work more consciously than we have been doing;

and that if we do, some of our behaviors will change and some of our results will improve.

For example: If I bring five percent more consciousness to my work—

I'd procrastinate less.
I'd think more about my priorities.
I'd get more done.
I wouldn't waste time on pointless conversations.
I'd stay focused on the most important issues.
I'd be less confused about what to do.
I'd accomplish more with less effort.
I'd finish my work on time.
I'd learn more about what's going on around me and wouldn't feel so isolated.
I'd look for ways to do more than I was asked to do.
I'd learn more about the business.
I'd grow more.
I'd be less restless.
I'd have more energy.
work would be more stimulating.
I wouldn't put off necessary phone calls.
I'd be straighter with my boss.
I'd get more accomplished.

One advantage of such an exercise is that, through it, people experience as a personal discovery, as knowledge generated from within, the significance of operating more (or less) consciously— rather than as information asserted by someone else in a lecture. Thus the awareness is both immediate and personal.

▲▲▲

It is generally recognized that in our modern information economy, a far higher level of knowledge, education, and skills is required of employees than was true in the past. What is less well understood is that what is also required is a much higher level of self-esteem, self-responsibility, *and mindfulness.*

▼

Walk into an average office and it is not difficult to see substantial differences in the level of consciousness at which different people operate. There are people who function at a heightened level of awareness, people who project a very modest level, and sometimes someone who projects that awareness itself (at almost any level) is a burden and an imposition. Generally speaking, it is not a mystery why some people advance rapidly in an organization while others barely manage to keep their jobs. One person actively seeks to learn everything he or she can about the business, looks for ways to work better and more productively, seeks to take on new challenges and responsibilities as a path to growth and advancement. Another person's vision may extend no further than the literal job description; that individual does what he or she is told to do, has little or no curiosity about the wider context of the work, no drive to learn, and wants promotions and rewards determined by seniority. Another person may feel that a job is something owed to him or her by "the system," and that consciousness is largely an after-hours activity—if it is to be bothered with at all. (What is the level of consciousness of those "egalitarians" who insist that all three types of individuals are equally deserving —and who protest the economic inequalities of their rewards in a free market society?)

It is generally recognized that in our modern information economy, a far higher level of knowledge, education, and skills is required of employees than was true in the past. What is less well understood is that what is also required is a much higher level of self-esteem, self-responsibility, *and mindfulness*. Organizations today need people who are willing and able to think, act on their own initiative, exercise independent judgment, be creative, and take responsibility for solving more and more of the problems that confront them without referring those problems to "higher-ups." The muscle-worker has largely been replaced by the knowledge-worker. This means that, to be economically adaptive, we need to be not merely able-bodied but *able-minded*—to bring a high level of consciousness to our tasks. Historically, the need for this mentality in large numbers rather than in a handful of exceptions is an unprecedented phenomenon. It is a development that has profound implications for our child-rearing practices, our educational system, and the values that will have to be dominant in our culture —values that serve and celebrate autonomy, innovativeness, self-responsibility, *consciousness* (in contrast to such traditional values as obedience, conformity, respect for authority). New technological and economic realities may be driving our evolution as a species, commanding us to rise to a higher level than our ancestors. If this premise is correct, it is the most important development of the twentieth century—and, in its ramifications, the least appreciated.

▲ ▲ ▲

**Only a policy of continuous learning, applied
over a lifetime, can allow one to remain
economically adaptive.**

▼

In the past, one received training in one's craft, trade, or profession, achieved a basic level of competence, and then spent the rest of one's working life applying what one had learned. In few fields of endeavor is this still possible. Today, when the sum total of human knowledge is said to be doubling roughly every ten years, knowledge becomes obsolete very quickly. What was learned yesterday is inadequate to tomorrow's needs. Only a policy of continuous learning, pursued over a lifetime, can allow one to remain economically adaptive. Access to decent jobs depends on this policy. No one can be said to be working consciously who imagines that he or she has thought and learned "enough."

Life has always meant growth, but never so obviously as today. Not to move forward is to move backward. Not to be expanding in consciousness is to be contracting. The employees with the brightest futures are those who, having mastered the challenges of today, are studying to meet the challenges of tomorrow. These are the men and women for whom learning is not a response to crisis but a way of life.

The principle that applies to individuals applies equally to corporations. We hear a great deal today about the need for businesses to be "learning organizations." No enterprise can afford to imagine it has learned enough or innovated enough. Continuous innovation is an imperative of survival in a fiercely competitive global economy. And since an organization is only a group of individuals working toward a common goal, its economic performance depends, ultimately, on how conscious and conscientious and self-responsible are the people it employs—and how conscious and conscientious and self-responsible they are *encouraged* to be and *rewarded* for being by the business's internal culture.

If schools are to play their part in preparing young people for the demands of the world they will enter, enormous emphasis must be placed on teaching how to think, how to learn, and how to function self-responsibly. And incidentally, *this* is how one nurtures self-esteem (at the same time as one builds competence), *not* by having children sing songs about how special they are or by having them wear badges that proudly proclaim "I am unique." (A hay sandwich is also unique.)

Yet another change from the past that bears on the intensified need to operate consciously is the fact that it is no longer possible to believe security is guaranteed if one has a good job with a large company and does one's job well. The devastating setbacks of seemingly impregnable businesses and the massive layoffs of the past two decades have exploded that assumption. In addition, in many cases new technologies made old jobs superfluous. In other cases, jobs were lost because of restructuring or downsizing (sometimes reflecting wise and necessary economic decisions on the part of management, sometimes done out of unthinking panic, with no resulting benefits to the business). In any event, what was destroyed was the illusion that "if you're loyal to the company, the company will be loyal to you and take care of you." (Even in Japan that notion is falling apart.) To the extent that employees thought about the issue, it became clear that the only real source of security in this world lay in their own knowledge, skills, and competence —which they could carry with them from one job to another.

Further, when people worked for the same company for several decades, they usually did not do much independent thinking about their career. A career path was laid out by the company. The situation is very different now. Today, even within an organization, more and more people are called on to, in effect, create their own jobs, carve out their own niches, plan their own futures, seek out the training they will need to get them to the next level of their ambitions and interests. And even more so is this the case when over the years one changes employment several times, moving from company to company, loyal primarily not to any particular organization but to one's own profession, trade, or craft—and carrying along the knowledge and ability that represent one's most important wealth.

All these changes require a higher level of self-reliance and self-responsibility than was asked for previously—and this means a higher, more active level of mindfulness. In the words of T. George Harris, ours is "an era of conscious action."[4]

To grasp this fact fully and think through its implications for one's own life is itself an act of high consciousness.

In response to the needs of corporate clients, I have designed a number of sentence-completion programs aimed at different aspects of raising performance. I reproduce below one such consciousness-expanding program. In terms of producing dramatic, bottom-line results, it is one of the most successful I have ever developed.

A Sentence-Completion Program to Facilitate High Performance

Sentence-completion work is a deceptively simple yet uniquely powerful tool for raising self-understanding, self-esteem, and personal and professional effectiveness. It rests on the premise that all of us have more resources than we normally are aware of, more potentials than ordinarily show up in our behavior. Sentence completion is a tool for accessing and activating these unrecognized resources. When we intensify awareness, we tend to generate a need for action that expresses our changed psychological state.

While sentence completion can be used for many different purposes, here we are focused on improving effectiveness in the workplace. For one person, this will mean bringing a higher level of motivation to the job. For another, being more innovative and creative. For another, being more skillful in interpersonal encounters. For another, breaking new records in sales. For another, starting a fire under career ambition. For another, simply making more money. Or any combination of the foregoing.

The essence of the procedure, as we will use it here, is to write an incomplete sentence, a sentence stem, and to keep adding different endings. The sole requirements are that each ending grammatically complete the sentence and that each ending be different. You can write in a notebook or work with a computer.

Work as rapidly as possible. No pauses to "think" (rehearse, calculate, censor); no worrying about whether any particular end-

113

ing is profound, relevant, or significant. Later, reflect on what you have written, by all means, but do not think in the instant before writing. Allow yourself to be surprised by what comes out of you. If you get stuck for an ending, invent.

For each stem, write a minimum of six endings; more is better. An average session should not take longer than ten minutes. If it takes much longer, you are "thinking" too much.

For each day of the week, Monday through Friday, there are four basic stems to be completed. These are done by everyone. There are two additional—optional—stems for people who want more concentration on sales or marketing or being an effective member of a team.

At the start of each day, before beginning work, do at least six endings for each stem. From day to day, inevitably there will be repetitions. That is not a problem, but do not allow repetitions on the same day.

WEEK 1

If I take full responsibility for my standard of living—
If I take full responsibility for my choices and actions—
If I bring a high level of awareness to my work life—
If I look at my work life realistically—
   For people in sales and marketing:
If I think of the customer as my partner—
   For people who work in teams:
If I think of all team members as my partners—

Then, in the evening, after the day's work and before dinner, do the following stem:

When I reflect on what I've noticed today—

WEEK 2

If I look at how I spend my time—
When I reflect on the level of awareness I bring to my work life—
If I think about how I set my priorities—
If I think about how I invest my time—

Sales and marketing:
If I want to keep a customer for life—
Team:
If I want to be perceived as an effective team player—
Evening:
When I reflect on what I've noticed today—

WEEK 3

If I were to commit myself to achieving greater financial success—
If I were willing to work using everything I know—
If I reflect on what it means to take full responsibility for my
standard of living—
If I reflect on how it might feel to commit myself fully to financial
success—
Sales and marketing:
A really innovative approach to my work might include—
Team:
A really innovative approach to my work might entail—
Evening:
When I reflect on what I've noticed today—

WEEK 4

If I reflect on what it means to use everything I know—
If I take full responsibility for my choices and actions—
If I take full responsibility for how I deal with people—
If I remain in full mental focus every moment today—
Sales and marketing:
If I want customers to trust and admire our company—
Team:
If I were convinced what I do makes a difference—
Evening:
When I reflect on what I've noticed today—

WEEK 5

If I reflect on what it means to take responsibility for my choices and
actions—

115

If I reflect on what it means to take responsibility for how I deal with people—
If I bring a higher level of awareness to my social anxieties—
If I reflect on what I would do if I remained in full mental focus at work today—
Sales and marketing:
If I were to do my job absolutely without fear—
Team:
If I want everyone in our team to pull together—
Evening:
When I reflect on what I've become aware of today—

WEEK 6

If I commit myself to raising my standard of living—
If I commit myself to a high level of success—
If I want to be more innovative in my work—
If I want to achieve a breakthrough in my work—
Sales and marketing:
If I want to raise my performance by ten percent—
Team:
If I want to contribute ten percent more to my team's efforts—
Evening:
When I reflect on what I've become aware of today—

WEEK 7

If I stay focused on the goal of being more successful—
If I treat listening as a creative act—
If I bring a higher level of purpose to my daily activities—
If I want to raise the level of my creativity—
Sales and marketing:
A new approach to selling might include—
Team:
Our team might be more effective if we—
Evening:
When I reflect on what I've become aware of today—

WEEK 8

If I notice how people are affected by the quality of my listening—
If I bring a higher level of self-responsibility to my daily activities—
If I bring a higher level of benevolence to my dealings with people—
If I want to be perceived as trustworthy—
Sales and marketing:
The scary thing about performing at a higher level is—
Team:
If I want my team members to feel accepted and respected by me—
Evening:
When I reflect on what I've become aware of today—

WEEK 9

If I am fully present to whoever is talking to me—
If I am fully present to whatever I am doing—
If I keep my career goals clearly in focus—
If I look for opportunities to contribute—
Sales and marketing:
If I want to translate my understandings into action—
Team:
If I want to translate my understandings into action—
Evening:
When I reflect on what I've become aware of today—

WEEK 10

If I treat myself with respect when dealing with other people—
If I treat other people with respect—
If I bring a higher level of integrity to all my dealings with people—
If I choose to set an example of personal integrity—
Sales and marketing:
One way to raise sales is—
Team:
If I want my associates to have confidence in me—
Evening:
When I reflect on what I've become aware of today—

WEEK 11

If I take success seriously as a goal—
If I stay focused and committed to greater success—
If I think of success as natural and appropriate to me—
If I breathe deeply and experience my own power—
Sales and marketing:
If I commit myself to raising my level of sales—
Team:
If I commit myself to a higher level of contribution—
Evening:
I am becoming aware—

WEEK 12

If I choose to give my best at work today—
If I bring a higher level of benevolence to whomever I deal with today—
If I want to convert my dreams into realities, I need to—
If I really want the life I say I want—
Sales and marketing:
If I want our customers to feel deeply attached to our company—
Team:
If I want our team to see me as a valued member—
Evening:
I am becoming aware—

WEEK 13

If I tap into a power within me I've never fully used—
If I pay more attention to how I deal with people today—
If I want to bring more clarity and purpose to my work today—
If I bring a higher level of enthusiasm to my work today—
Sales and marketing:
If I bring more benevolence to my interactions with people—
Team:
If I bring more benevolence to my dealings with team members—
Evening:
I am becoming aware—

WEEK 14

If I operate as if my work will determine the success or failure of my company—
If I want to take more pleasure in my work, I will—
If I want to take more pride in my work, I will—
If I want to operate more self-responsibly at work, I will—
Sales and marketing:
If I can accept operating at a higher level—
Team:
If I want to be a superb team player—
Evening:
I am becoming aware—

WEEK 15

If I approach my work as an opportunity for self-development—
If I bring a higher level of self-esteem to my work—
If I want to make it easier and more pleasant for others to deal with me—
If I give people the experience of being seen and heard by me—
Sales and marketing:
If I want to be more creative in my work—
Team:
If I want to contribute more to my team—
Evening:
If any of what I am writing is true, it might be helpful if—

WEEK 16

If I bring a higher level of consciousness to my work today—
If I bring a higher level of benevolence to my dealings with people today—
If I operate at a higher level of self-responsibility today—
If I bring more integrity to my work today—
Sales and marketing:
If I bring a higher level of consciousness to our clients or customers—

Team:
If I bring a higher level of consciousness to my team interactions—
Evening:
If any of what I'm writing is true, it might be helpful if—

WEEK 17

If I bring a higher level of purposefulness to my work today—
If I operate more self-assertively today—
If I want to break through to a higher level of performance in my work today—
If I want my work to bring me more joy—
Sales and marketing:
If I want to bring more excitement to my work—
Team:
If I want to bring more excitement to our team—
Evening:
If any of what I've written is true, it might be helpful if—

WEEK 18

If I look for challenges to my creativity today—
If I look for challenges to my resourcefulness today—
If I bring a higher level of excitement to my work—
If I want to feel more pride in my work—
Sales and marketing:
As I keep expanding my vision of what is possible to me—
Team:
If I keep expanding my vision of what is possible to me—
Evening:
If any of what I've written is true, it might be helpful if—

WEEK 19

If I take full responsibility for the attainment of my desires—
I feel most proud of myself at work when—
If I commit myself at work to using everything I know—
If I treat my goals and aspirations with respect—

Sales and marketing:
If I want to operate at a high level of motivation—
Team:
If I want to help energize my team—
Evening:
If any of what I've written is true, it might be helpful if—

WEEK 20
If I accept success as natural and appropriate to me—
If my self-concept expands to a higher vision of my possibilities—
If I fully deserve whatever I am able to earn—
As I grow more comfortable with higher levels of performance—
Sales and marketing:
If I can see myself as a much higher level producer—
Team:
One of the things my team needs from me is—
Evening:
If any of what I've written is true, it might be helpful if—

I will not attempt, in this context, to discuss the reasoning behind the structure of the sentences or the design of the progression. I will only say that those who work with this program consistently report a significant expansion of awareness combined with enhanced motivation and improved performance. What the program demonstrates in action is the energizing power of awareness in the workplace.

CONSCIOUSNESS OF CONTEXT

▲ ▲ ▲
**One measure of our mindfulness is the extent
to which we are even aware of the issue of our
context and the nature of its effects on us.**
▼

No one exists in a vacuum. We live in a neighborhood, a society, a country, a world. We live in a physical environment, a social environment, a cultural/intellectual environment, and a political environment. We live on a street—and on a planet. More forces —material and spiritual—are impinging on us than it is possible to be aware of. We are affected by our world in more ways than we can register consciously. But one measure of our mindfulness is the extent to which we are even aware of the issue of our context and the nature of its effects on us.

To what extent does it occur to us even to reflect on the countless factors that touch on and sometimes influence our life?

I once suggested to a passionate religionist, who had accepted from his parents that theirs was the one true religion, that if he had been born in India, he might feel the same way about Hinduism. My point was not that our family context necessarily determines our religious beliefs (it doesn't), but that if in one context he had accepted on the authority of his parents one set of beliefs, in different circumstances he could accept another. "I cannot even imagine such a thing," he answered. "I hear what you're saying, but it has no reality for me. I just cannot believe it."

Irrespective of what we notice explicitly, all of us are affected by the world in which we live—physically, culturally, socially, economically, politically. The physical environment has consequences for our health. The cultural environment affects our attitudes, values, and the pleasure we take or cannot take in what we see, hear, and read. The social environment may have an effect on the serenity or turbulence of our existence. Economic factors affect our standard of living. Political factors affect the measure of our freedom and the extent of our control over our lives. And this list is far from exhaustive.

Consider, for example, what we might term the "spiritual environment." The twentieth century has been one of unprecedented horror in the amount of violence and destruction human beings have perpetrated against one another. The sheer amount of human-caused suffering in this century is beyond the mind's ability to hold in a single focus. I have long felt that we have all been spiritually affected by this—poisoned is not too strong a word—in ways difficult to fully articulate or prove. It is as if the air we breathe is itself contaminated with the cries and agonies of countless millions, as if the cells of our bodies register their screams even when our ears hear nothing.

To be oblivious to all these forces, to imagine that we live in a vacuum, is truly to live as a sleepwalker.

Will differences in intelligence affect what a person is likely to be conscious of in these areas? Of course. A person of high intelligence with a philosophical disposition may be sensitive to far more than a person of more limited intellect. But even among persons of modest powers, we can discern differences in interest level with regard to these matters—differences in curiosity, thoughtfulness, awareness that there is something about which to think. If our intention is to operate mindfully, these are matters on which we need to reflect. Such reflection is an integral aspect of a conscious existence.

Notice, for example, how your spirit is affected by watching the morning news or reading a newspaper. Observe the spiritual impact on you of the people, actions, and stories portrayed in movies and television. What sense of life is evoked? What sense of human beings are you left with? What conclusions, if any, do you draw from what you see and hear?

Many people, when they encounter the idea of shifting to a higher level of consciousness, immediately associate it with the mystical, religious, or supernatural. I do not. I associate it with paying greater attention to the here and now—often to what is staring us in the face—undistorted by our wishes, fears, or preconceptions. *This earth* is the distant star we must find a way to reach. And all of the foregoing discussion in this chapter and the preceding ones is only a series of examples of what this means.

CONSCIOUSNESS OF OUR IDEAS AND THEIR ROOTS

Implicitly, if not explicitly, all of us have what amounts to a philosophy of life. That is to say, we operate from assumptions or convictions concerning a wide variety of issues—human nature, man/woman relationships, sexuality and gender issues, psychology and motivation, ethics and accountability, art and entertainment, politics and economics. However, we may not always be conscious of our beliefs. Or we may not be conscious of how we arrived at them—whether, for example, we absorbed them from others by osmosis, generated them unthinkingly out of our emotions, or arrived at them by a process of rational thought or by a mixture of processes, part rational, part not.

About most of their beliefs, most people are poorly prepared to answer the questions, How did you arrive at that conclusion? What are the perceptions, experiences, reasoning on which your beliefs are based?

When I was sixteen years old, a relative asked me what profession I planned to pursue, and I answered psychology. The year was 1946, and in the world I inhabited, few people knew what such a field entailed. To set the context for her response, I should mention that I was living in Toronto, where winters can be quite cold. She responded, as if she were saying the most obvious, noncontroversial thing imaginable, "That's ridiculous. There's no money in psychology. A man's job is to earn a decent living so he can buy his wife a fur coat and take her to Florida in the winter." (This statement is verbatim, to the best of my recollection.) "Why?" I asked her, fascinated even then by what she took as self-evident. She replied, "Oh, *please*. Don't be silly."

A few years ago, I was at a dinner party where the discussion turned to politics. Most of the people appeared to be Democrats, but the woman sitting next to me was a Republican. (I am neither; I am a classical liberal, which in twentieth-century terms means a libertarian, one who upholds the supremacy of individual rights and a minimalist role for government.) At one point, the Republican woman, responding to the mention of a prominent business-man, made the following offhand statement: "Well, you know nobody gets to be the CEO of a major corporation who ever lets scruples or ethics stand in his way. They're all crooks." No one challenged her; they greeted her remark as if it were too obviously true to require comment. Republicans, I thought, amused, were presumed to be champions of business. (They are not; notice, for example, the attacks on wealth and "big business" by most of the Republican contenders for their party's presidential nomination in 1996—conveying to the nation that somehow the mere possession of wealth makes one morally suspect.) Knowing this woman's allegation to be absurd, I said, "What an extraordinary observation. Tell me, how many CEOs of major corporations do you personally know? You're making quite a serious accusation—and not just about one man but about a whole group. What is it based on? How did you arrive at your belief?" There was a frozen silence, as if I had committed a social gaffe. When the woman stared at me resentfully, without answering, the hostess broke the silence by saying brightly, "That's why they say there's two subjects one shouldn't discuss at parties—religion and politics."

▲ ▲ ▲

As adults, we may come to regard an
appalling level of unconsciousness as normal.
Instead, we must ask: *What are my grounds
for holding the views I hold?*

▼

One of the characteristics of living consciously is that we seek to understand the reasons for our beliefs—and are not resentful or defensive if someone asks us to name them.

If we are unable to name them, as may sometimes happen, conscious (and intellectually conscientious) men and women acknowledge that fact and take responsibility for it. They do not make it the occasion of an angry counterattack or supercilious silence and withdrawal.

One of the characteristics of people who operate unconsciously in the realm of ideas is that they feel entitled to hold positions on all kinds of subjects—without information, knowledge, study, or thought, as if their "intuitions" and "instincts" were all they needed. Three fields where this tendency is particularly prevalent are religion, politics, and psychology.

When we are young and struggling toward autonomy, the more intellectually active among us ask a great many "whys." We want to know why adults assert the things they do. We demand reasons. Later, worn out by too many disappointing human encounters— by too many answers that are not answers—we may lose the fire to persist with this inquiry. People's beliefs, including our own, may acquire the status of primaries, irreducible facts, about which no questions are to be asked. Intellectual passion may be replaced by intellectual lethargy. We may come to view philosophical thinking with contempt. We may surrender to the anesthetic of unconsciousness, while telling ourselves it is wisdom (or even "higher awareness").

As adults, we may come to regard an appalling level of unconsciousness as normal.

And in that state—to cite only one illustration from the realm of politics—we can vote for politicians whose policies send thousands of young men to senseless death, expropriate property, destroy businesses, stifle innovation, penalize ability and success, crush ambition, discourage self-responsibility, reward dependency, destroy families, and fuel the escalation of crime.

In the realm of politics, how can one intelligently decide which candidate to support or which program to endorse if one has no intellectual frame of reference in which to place the issues? If they are to be more than emotional expressions, political judgments need to rest on a set of deeper convictions about the proper nature of government, the relationship of the individual to the state, the question of whether human beings are ends in themselves or may be treated as means to the ends of others, the meaning of justice, and a good many other ethical issues. And all these questions lead to a still deeper question: *What are my grounds for holding the views I hold?* ("Because it's what my heart tells me" is not an answer.) A genuine concern with such issues is what it means to operate consciously in the political arena—what it means, for example, to vote consciously or to legislate consciously.

Can we attempt to function mindfully and yet err in our judgments? Of course. We are not infallible. But if we choose to remain conscious and to continually look for evidence that confirms or disconfirms our judgment—*if we continue to think, to be open to reality, and to be undefensive*—sooner or later we may become alerted to our mistakes. If, instead, we sink into unconsciousness about our convictions, reality may be trying to reach us, but we have left the receiver off the hook.

All of us sometimes draw mistaken or irrational conclusions from our experience, on the basis of which we form values harmful to our well-being. A young person may see many examples of dishonesty and hypocrisy while growing up, may conclude, in effect, "This is the way the world works, and I must adapt to it," and may, as a consequence, disvalue honesty and integrity. Of course, such a mistake cannot be reconciled with living consciously —not in the long run, at any rate—but it is only the rigor of our thinking that can guard against such mistakes.

All of us absorb values from the world around us—from family, peers, and culture—and those values are not necessarily rational or supportive of our true interests; often, in fact, they are not. A man may permit himself to absorb the idea of identifying personal worth with income; a woman may permit herself to absorb the idea of identifying personal worth with the social or financial status of the man she marries. To the extent we attempt to live as thinking beings, we have the possibility of protection against such errors; if we attempt to exist as unthinking conformists, we have no such protection—we are truly at the mercy of our environment.

For this reason, parents who love their children with wisdom and not merely with feeling encourage independent, critical thinking. They teach them that the unexamined idea is not worth holding.

It might be argued that no one could possibly examine all the ideas he or she is influenced or moved by. This is true—but irrelevant. No one can be flawlessly reasonable all the time, but this does not mean it is futile to strive to be reasonable. No one can be perfectly just all the time, but if we have integrity, we do attempt to be as just as we know how to be. No one can be consistently kind on all occasions—or even be certain of what true kindness consists in some cases—but still, *we try to raise our average.*

▲ ▲ ▲

Mindfulness is an orientation, a discipline, a spiritual commitment. It is the direction in which we aim, the path to which we pledge our lives.

▼

To live consciously means that in the different areas of life, we seek to be aware and to act in accordance with our awareness. It does not mean we will always succeed. Mindfulness is an orientation, a discipline, a spiritual commitment. It is the direction in which we aim, the path to which we pledge our lives.

Consciousness is our basic tool for successful adaptation to reality. The more conscious we are in any situation, the more possibilities we tend to perceive; therefore, the more options we have; therefore, the more powerful we are. The less conscious we are in any given situation, the fewer the possibilities that occur to us; therefore, the more rigid and mechanical are our responses; therefore, the less effective we are. Nothing is more practical than mindfulness.

Self-Awareness: Examining Our Inner World

"WHAT are you feeling right now?" I asked Audrey W., a fifty-year-old pharmacist.

"I really don't know," she answered.

"Can you feel the tears on your cheeks?" I inquired.

Audrey paused thoughtfully, then said, "Yes, I guess I can."

"Are you aware that you're crying?"

"Yes, I guess I am."

"What's that about?"

"I really don't know."

"Well, let me ask you this. If your eyes had a soul and feelings of their own, what might they be feeling right now?"

"Oh," Audrey answered without hesitation, "sadness. Deep, deep sadness. And grief."

"Do you think it could be *you* who is experiencing deep sadness and grief?"

"Oh, yes," she said urgently, "yes, yes, yes." She began to weep again. "I am so unhappy."

Some readers may find this story unusual, but no psychotherapist will, since he or she deals frequently with extreme instances of non-self-awareness. To protect against pain, people have the ability to disown and repress feelings—when those feelings threaten equilibrium. In other words, they induce unconsciousness, which is what Audrey had done.

Wanting to give Audrey a safe corridor through which she could approach her feared feelings, I invited momentary disassociation from her own experience, suggesting that not Audrey but *her eyes* had the feelings, and then the layer of denial was broken and she was able to recognize and admit the obvious fact of her unhappiness. Of course, the process of uncovering may be much more difficult than as described in this vignette—or it may not—it may be just as simple. (Sometimes I will ask clients, "What emotion is your heart—or chest or stomach or legs or whatever—experiencing right now?"—to help them identify a feeling they are not yet prepared to own directly. And most of the time they will answer.)

To disown means to cease to recognize as our own. We can be alienated from—inadequately conscious of—our bodies, our needs and wants, our feelings and emotions, our actions and reactions, our thoughts and values, or our abilities and capacities. We can be strangers to ourselves in many different possible respects. We can act without recognizing the roots of our actions. We can be afraid without knowing what we are afraid of and long without knowing what we are longing for. These are some of the meanings of self-alienation and self-disowning.

A consequence of this process is that we radically restrict our sense of self. We have less access to our inner signals, and consequently we become more dependent on signals from others. We may need others to tell us what to think, how to live, when to express which emotion (if at all), what is right or wrong, and so forth.

At minimum, we pay a price in suffering, when we are inappropriate in our responses and frustrated in our life. But sometimes we pay even a worse price, as when, for instance—"What stress are you talking about?" asks a driven, workaholic salesman of forty-eight a moment before he drops dead of a heart attack.

No one can be said to be living consciously who exempts self-examination from the agenda. So let us look at some of the key areas to which self-awareness pertains.

CONSCIOUSNESS OF THE BODY

Western culture for many centuries has tended to encourage alienation from the body. The body has been perceived as a source of sin, luring one away from one's higher nature—the traditional religious perspective. Or it has been perceived as a servant that has duties to perform and little right to feelings, little right to have its pain or weariness given serious consideration—or else as a machine, with the same obligations—the traditional Puritan work-ethic perspective. Or it has been perceived as an esoteric mystery that only experts can understand, while the person inhabiting the body is not presumed to know anything about it worth knowing —the traditional medical perspective.[1] (Regarding this last, studies disclose that any number of medical mistakes are traceable to physicians' disinclination to *listen to their patients*.)

It is a major step in an infant's development to recognize the body as its own and to grasp where body ends and the external world begins. It is a higher step to grasp that one is more than one's body, as a more complex concept of self evolves. But once this possibility is actualized, a new danger presents itself: that of *disassociation* from the body.

Many factors in a young person's life experiences can encourage this disassociation. A child can see the body as a source of parental irritation and even revulsion if, for example, Mother conveys disgust in the way she bathes or touches it. Or perhaps a child becomes ill and begins to hate the body as a source of suffering and betrayal. Or a child sees a loved one sicken and die, and again the body is perceived as a traitor—especially if and when death is perceived as unnatural or somehow a failure of life. In adolescence, the body may be perceived as the sinful source or repository of sexual longings and therefore of guilt. In school, a young person's mind/body split may be exacerbated through physical education teachers who see the body as an object to be beaten into performing, to be controlled and manipulated. He or she may be taught to override bodily signals of pain or to become unconscious of them. There is growing evidence that any number of unnecessary accidents and injuries among professional and amateur athletes and dancers are the consequence of inappropriate practice and training methods that reflect a perspective of body-as-adversary. In a high-pressure work environment, again the perspective of body-as-adversary has reached epidemic proportions. It is a very short step from body-as-adversary to body-blocked-from-consciousness.

Fortunately, the tide may be turning. More and more people today are learning respect for their body and its signals, are taking more responsibility for its care and maintenance, and are generally bringing more consciousness to the physical domain. However, in terms of optimal body consciousness, we have a very long way to go. Abuse of our bodies and obliviousness to its messages are still more the norm than the exception.

One of the areas in which alienation from the body is most evident is the sexual. Studies demonstrate that a woman can have an orgasm while denying she is experiencing anything in particular, so blocked is she from her own pelvic sensations. Sometimes, working with a woman who is dissociated from her body in this way, I ask her to perform bump-and-grind movements while saying aloud, over and over again, "I am a good girl." The exercise is a multilevel assault on the problem. Physically, the movements induce some relaxation in the pelvic musculature, increase blood circulation, and thereby raise the level of feeling. Psychologically, the physical movements are a complete repudiation of her childhood training, while the ironic humor of "I am a good girl" interrupts her routine thought patterns and releases her to a fresh perspective. Sometimes, as the client begins to feel an increase of sensation in the pelvic area, anxiety arises, and she makes direct contact with the fear of disapproval that inspired the original blocking. As she is encouraged not to fight but to accept the anxiety, it tends to disappear, and what she progressively experiences is a sense of liberation and excitement—the sense *of waking up.*

There is a sense in which our entire body can be viewed as part of our brain—that is, it contains and processes information, stores shocks and traumas to which the conscious mind is oblivious, and influences our emotions and thoughts. Notice how something as simple as a bad cold can affect our feelings and emotions. A long-forgotten childhood trauma—say, a physical beating or an act of sexual molestation—whose imprint is left not only in the subconscious but also in the body itself can affect an adult's ability to handle intimacy: he or she may experience a disabling fear that the body has been carrying for decades.

I will have more to say about the body (and body-as-brain) as we examine the sphere of feelings and emotions. But here are a few examples of how one can use sentence-completion work to facilitate greater body awareness. What follows are incomplete sentences I use in my practice—and typical endings:

If I brought five percent more awareness to my body—

I'd know when I was tired.

I'd take better care of myself.

I wouldn't get sick so often.

I'd recognize what foods aren't good for me.

I'd face how much pain I haven't dealt with.

I'd recognize how much I know without knowing that I know.

I'd be more sensitive to other people's moods and feelings.

I'd live more in the moment.

I wouldn't rush by so fast.

I'd be quicker to know when I'm hurt or angry.

I wouldn't bury so many feelings.

I'd be more sexual.

I'd want more.

I'd feel more alive.

I'd be more here.

I'd see how much information is available to me.

I'd experience more of my body's messages.

I'd know my body better.

I'd better understand my body's signals.

CONSCIOUSNESS OF OUR NEEDS AND WANTS

When I invite clients in psychotherapy to talk about their needs and wants, what often impresses me is how awkward, hesitant, and helpless they become. Rarely do they answer clearly and explicitly. It is often as if they are struggling against some internal prohibition that forbids them to know or state what their deepest needs and wants are. Yet how can one live or act effectively without knowing?

There are several possible reasons for this problem. One is that as children they received parental messages that amounted to, "Listen, kid, here is the news. Life is not about you. Life is not about what you need or want or feel. It is about what other people need or want or feel. You don't really matter." Another is that when a child's needs and wants are too often ignored, the pain feels too much to bear—and so, in self-protection, as a survival strategy, the child learns to repress his or her needs and wants, to bury them outside of awareness, seeking unconsciousness as a refuge. Another is that one kind of trauma or another may lead a child to experience life as so frightening, so dangerous, that any form of self-assertiveness is stifled—even the self-assertiveness of merely *knowing* (let alone expressing) what one needs and wants. Another is that we may experience certain desires that clash with our self-concept, and so we deny and disown them—for example, a grown man's need for physical nurturing, for simple holding and stroking, that he will not permit himself to acknowledge because it clashes with his idea of manliness and autonomy; so, again, the problem is "solved" by unconsciousness.

▲ ▲ ▲

**Honoring one's true wants can be not an act of
self-indulgence but an act of courage.**

▼

One way or the other, important needs and wants often get buried alive. This does not mean they cease to exist. It merely means they affect our feelings and behavior in ways we do not recognize. For example, the disowned need for physical touch and nurturing may show up as compulsive sexual promiscuity, since sex is the only acceptable form of physical touch the man recognizes. Or the need for understanding and visibility that is a child's birthright may show up in an adult's obsession with being "pleasing" and "popular," often in ways that are humiliating and offensive to self-esteem.

For these reasons, I often work with such stems as "If I bring five percent more consciousness to my deepest needs—" followed by "If I bring five percent more consciousness to my deepest longings—" followed by "If someone had taught me my needs and wants mattered—" followed by "If I treat my needs and wants with respect—" We might see a pattern of responses like this:

If I bring five percent more consciousness to my deepest needs—

I would know what they are.
Mother wouldn't approve.
I could take better care of myself.
I've never done that.
I wouldn't be so confused.
I wouldn't be so angry at other people for not guessing what I need.
I'd have to face how lonely I am.
I'd know about my soul hunger.

If I bring five percent more consciousness to my deepest longings—

I'd know that the work I'm doing isn't enough.
I'd have to face how much I've missed in life because I was afraid to
    go after it.
I'd begin playing the piano again.
I'd try to write.
I'd go back to school.
I'd read more, whether my partner is interested or not.
I'd quit my job and start my own business.
I'd know how one-dimensional my life is.

If someone had taught me my needs and wants mattered—

that would be someone else's childhood, not mine.
my whole life would be different.
I wouldn't be in therapy.
I would have created a life.
I'd have fought for something.
I wouldn't have stayed, out of guilt, with a man I don't love.
I'd treat them as important.
my whole life wouldn't be duty and obligation.
I wouldn't have believed people about the beauty of sacrifice.
I would have thought more about what really mattered to me.

If I treat my needs and wants with respect—

that's frightening.
Mother would have a heart attack.
no one would like me.
I wouldn't have any friends.
I'd have *self*-respect.

it would take courage.
people would say I'm selfish.
I wouldn't care what people think.
I'd be a human being with dignity.

I think the significance of these endings, encountered again and again, is fairly obvious. No deep "interpretations" are necessary, only a little thoughtful reflection. Take a moment and imagine you are in a consulting room hearing such sentence completions. What conclusions would you come to? Would you see, perhaps, that honoring one's true wants can be not an act of self-indulgence but an act of courage?

▲ ▲ ▲

When we are out of contact with our needs and wants,
we face life disarmed and rudderless.

▼

Working with people in therapy, one has many opportunities to see how false is the idea that "it's easy to be selfish, but self-sacrifice is difficult." To treat needs and wants with decent respect, to fight for one's deepest longings, to take those longings *seriously,* is for many people a formidable and frightening challenge. To bury one's desires, to surrender even the ability to recognize them—to practice self-sacrifice in the *literal* sense—is often much easier. People give away pieces of their soul every day in order to escape responsibility—or to "belong." They are experts at this kind of self-surrender and self-sacrifice. If *selflessness* is the ideal, they are its walking, mutilated exponents. Then, in defiant resentment, not even knowing who or what they are defying, they become "selfish" not in the intelligent and noble but in the narrow and petty sense. (Sometimes the tragedy is compounded when moralists tell them, as cure for their suffering, not that they should learn intelligent self-respect but that they should lose themselves in service to others. And then the coffin of their self is sealed.)

When we are out of contact with our needs and wants, we face life disarmed and rudderless. Our unconsciousness is dangerous—to ourselves and often to others. We are blind to the roots of our actions. We are moved by forces we do not understand.

In our state of psychic numbness, we may even imagine that our disconnection from self represents the "spirituality of detachment," but a spirituality achieved by unconsciousness is a contradiction in terms.

CONSCIOUSNESS OF OUR FEELINGS AND EMOTIONS

We are not born with an ego or a sense of self. Both emerge and evolve over time. Essential to this process is the discovery of *separateness*—grasping boundaries, learning where we end and the world begins. Among other aspects of growth, this pertains to the unfolding of our emotional life.

For example, an infant, whose psychological identity is still in an early stage of development, experiences feelings and emotions before it is able to grasp that they are its own: the distinction between self and others has not fully been made. When it is able clearly to make that differentiation and to know that *these feelings and emotions belong to me*—it is *I* who am experiencing this—it takes an important step toward the full experience of selfhood.

This stage has been characterized as the formation of an "emotional self," which comes after an earlier stage in which the infant learns to distinguish its body as a separate entity in the world—the formation of a "body self," the foundation of all subsequent development.[2]

However, every step of development entails both new powers and new dangers. (For example, the ability to reason makes possible the ability to rationalize.) The danger once a child learns to recognize emotions as its own is that *it is now capable of blocking, disowning, and repressing emotions experienced as threatening.* The ability to say "This is me (or mine)" entails the ability to say "This is *not* me (or *not* mine)." Fear, rage, pain, sexuality—all can be cast out of awareness to protect the child's equilibrium and make life bearable. The door is thus open to the possibility of emotional self-alienation.

An emotion, in this context, refers to a psychophysiological response to some thought or perception. Thus it is both a mental and a physical event. It reflects an appraisal, typically subconscious, of the thought or perception to which we are responding. That is, it reflects an evaluation of the beneficial or harmful relationship of that thought or perception to ourselves. The value response involved will be on the order of "for me or against me," "good for me or harmful," "to be pursued or to be avoided."

Once an emotion arises, it tends to follow a natural course of its own: it is experienced, it is expressed in some form of bodily behavior, and it is discharged, to be replaced by some other emotion. This is the normal progression. When the process is blocked by denial or repression, unresolved tensions remain in the body— the emotion is dammed up, as it were—even if conscious awareness of the emotion has been extinguished or was never permitted to occur.

▲ ▲ ▲

We must *experience* and *acknowledge*—and
sometimes *examine* and *reflect on*—our
emotions for the sake of our well-being.
▼

Of course, not every emotion need be acted on. An emotion carries within it the impulse to perform some particular action (if only the action of remaining perfectly still), but emotion and action are different and distinct categories, and such impulses need not be obeyed blindly and uncritically. Sexual desire need not be translated into an act of sex. An angry impulse to strike someone need not be translated into an actual blow.

What we do require for our well-being, however, especially in the case of emotions that are more than superficial and momentary, is that we experience and *acknowledge them*—sometimes examine and reflect on them.

Whether our values and value judgments in any given situation are correct or mistaken and whether it is appropriate and possible to act on our feelings or not, our emotions do reflect the meaning that reality has for us at that time. So they need to be taken seriously. One does not destroy an emotion by refusing to feel it or acknowledge it; one merely disowns a part of oneself.

Our emotions are determined not merely by our values and beliefs in the abstract but also by our specific mental and physical state in a given moment. For example, if we are feeling healthy, vibrant, and effective, and receive a piece of bad news, we will not like it but nonetheless may remain cheerful and optimistic. On the other hand, if we receive the same news on a day when we are feeling weak, exhausted, or feverish, we may respond with an emotion of panic or depression. In either event, emotions inform us what things mean to us *if only in the moment.* Thus, to cease to know what we feel is to cease to experience the significance persons and events have for us. And this means in important respects *to be cut off from our own context*—which is a form of unconsciousness.

▲▼▲

How does this unconsciousness become built into our "operating system"? At the psychological level, one can more or less automatize the process of jerking one's mental focus away from emotions felt to be disturbing. At the physical level, this unconsciousness is induced by two means. One is restricting the breathing, reducing the intake of oxygen. For example, if we are suddenly frightened or startled, we typically breathe in sharply and freeze—stop breathing. We may characteristically block on the inhale or block on the exhale, depending on the particular emotion we are fighting. When repressing anger, for instance, we tend to block on the exhale. Every parent has noticed instances of a child suppressing crying by holding the breath. These responses too can become automatized, so that one is no longer aware of them. The second means by which repression is implemented physically is contracting the muscles that would be mobilized were the emotion fully felt *and expressed.* For example, people who block a lot of anger often have tightly contracted forearms, which would be used to strike were the anger fully released physically. Muscles repeatedly tensed against feeling eventually become chronically contracted. The contraction becomes part of one's physical structure. This is the body "armor" of which Wilhelm Reich wrote.

Today there are many forms of body therapy, most of which trace their roots to the work of Reich, that have as their aim freeing the body structure, freeing the breathing, so that the capacity to experience emotion deeply is regained.[3] What is important to understand is that this process is also *a freeing-up of consciousness.* When we repress emotion, we repress the value significance of events in the affected area, and thus we hamper our ability to think. Contrary to the notion that thought and emotion are intrinsic adversaries, the ability to feel deeply and without distortion supports the ability to think clearly, because one has access to pertinent information.

When parents convey that certain emotions are "unacceptable," they are teaching unconsciousness as the price of the child's retaining parental love and approval. A little boy falls and hurts himself and is told sternly by his father, "Men don't cry." First the little boy learns not to *show* when he is in pain and later, as the repression deepens, not to *know* when he is in pain. A little girl expresses anger at her brother or some other family member and is told by her mother, "It's terrible to feel that way. You don't *really* feel it." And the little girl's capacity to feel anger is not extinguished but merely buried beneath awareness, later in life to wreak bewildering havoc when it erupts in seemingly inexplicable contexts. A child bursts into the house, full of joy and excitement, and is told by an irritated parent, "What's wrong with you? Why must you make so much noise? Are you *crazy?*" And the child slowly absorbs the tragic notion that equates growing up with giving up the ability to experience excitement, which is one of a child's most sacred possessions.

We know that emotionally remote and inhibited parents—parents estranged from their own inner lives—tend to produce emotionally remote and inhibited children; not inevitably, perhaps, but very commonly. This is achieved not only by the parents' overt communications but also by the example they set. Their behavior implicitly announces to the child what is "proper," "appropriate," "socially acceptable," and what is not. And it is very easy for the child to internalize such messages.

If parents accept the notion of such things as "evil thoughts" or "evil emotions" and infect their child with this belief, a child may tie his or her self-esteem to having the "right" thoughts and feelings. This is a sure formula for inducing terror of one's inner life and motivation, to censor that which does not "fit"—to protect oneself with a shield of unconsciousness.

For too many children, the early years of life contain many frightening and painful experiences. Perhaps a child has parents who never respond to her need to be touched, held, and nurtured, who constantly scream at him or at each other, who deliberately evoke fear and guilt as a means of exercising control, who swing between oversolicitude and callous remoteness, who subject him to lies and mockery, who are neglectful and indifferent, who continually criticize and rebuke her, who overwhelm him with bewildering and contradictory injunctions, who present her with expectations that take no cognizance of her knowledge, needs, or interests, who subject him to physical violence, who sexually molest her, or who discourage his efforts at self-assertion. The child may experience his or her fear, pain, or anger as incapacitating. And so, in order to survive and be able to function, the child learns *psychic numbing.* Unobstructed contact with his or her inner state feels unbearable and dangerous. *Consciousness* feels unbearable and dangerous.

The fear, pain, and anger are not permitted to be recognized, experienced, expressed, and thus discharged. Instead, they are frozen into the body, barricaded behind walls of muscular and physiological tension. And a pattern is installed that will occur again and again when he or she is threatened by an emotion that disturbs the equilibrium of numbness.

Here is a simple, undramatic example of the common repression of childhood pain:

One evening many years ago, I was sitting with a group of psychologists and psychiatrists. I volunteered the thought, which by then I thought obvious, that large numbers of "normal" people carried within them a good deal of unresolved childhood suffering that remained a living, if unconfronted, issue within them. A young psychiatrist—Ian S.—challenged me, insisting I was exaggerating the pervasiveness of the problem.

I asked if he would be willing to cooperate in a demonstration, an "experiment" we would perform. Ian laughed and said he would be glad to but that he was a poor subject, because he'd had an unusually happy childhood. His manner was open and carefree, if a bit diffident, and it was clear he was intelligent. He spoke a bit softly, as if uncertain what he had to say would be of interest. I said I'd like to proceed with him, and he agreed.

I explained I had developed an exercise often useful in accessing painful or even traumatic childhood experiences, and which I proposed to demonstrate.

I asked him to sit back in his lounge chair, relax his body, let his hands rest at his sides, and close his eyes. "Now," I said, "I want you to imagine the following situation. You are lying on a bed in a hospital, and you are dying. You are your present age. You are not in physical pain, but you are aware of the fact that in a few hours your life will end. Now, in your imagination, look up and see your mother standing by the side of the bed. Look at her face." I paused, to allow him time to fully enter this reality. "Feel the presence of the unsaid—all the things you have never told her, all the thoughts and feelings you have never expressed. If ever you would be able to reach your mother, it is now. If ever she would hear you, it is now. Nothing to lose. Talk to her. Tell her what is was like to be her child."

As I was speaking, Ian's hands clenched into fists, blood rushed to his face, and one could see the muscular tension around his eyes and forehead that was aimed at suppressing tears. When he spoke, it was in a much younger voice than before, more intense, and his voice was a rising moan: "When I tried to talk to you, *why didn't you ever listen to me? . . . Why didn't you ever listen?*"

Since this was not a therapy session but a public demonstration, I chose to interrupt the process at that point; I did not want to violate his privacy. I knew if the exercise continued, he would get into issues he might prefer not to explore in this setting. After a moment he opened his eyes, shook his head, looked astonished and sheepish. His glance said that the point had been made.

Later, he acknowledged, "I'm shocked at how much sadness there is in me. So much pain. And a feeling of loneliness and isolation I never recognized. With all my training, it's incredible that this should come as news to me, and yet, right now, my whole life is looking different to me. . . . I can't yet explain in what way."

He wanted to know why I had chosen to have his mother by his bedside rather than his father, and I explained that in the full exercise, I did bring the father into the scene as well. What we had done was only the beginning of a lengthier process. I asked if he was aware he spoke in a rather diffident way, and when he said yes, I invited him to wonder if that diffidence might relate to not having been listened to as a child. (Some years later, when I began to work with subpersonalities, as described in *The Six Pillars of Self-Esteem,* I would have said that his child-self, the child he once was that still occupied space in his psyche, was controlling his manner of speaking.)

When he told me his childhood had been an unusually happy one, he had been sincere. The pain and the memory of what had caused it had been repressed long before. But the aftermath was not only an emotional impairment but also a thinking impairment, since any attempt he might have made to relate his past to his present or to understand his reticent personality would have been hampered by distorted judgments. He would have had no basis to understand some of his relationship problems as an adult. This is an example of the point that when we repress emotion, we restrict the clarity of thought.

We repress more than negative feelings. Repression as a pattern of response tends to embrace more and more of the emotional life. When one is given an anesthetic in preparation for surgery, it is not merely the capacity to experience pain that is suspended; the experience of pleasure goes also—because what is blocked is the capacity to experience *feeling.* Similarly with emotional repression.

Naturally, such repression is a matter of degree. In some individuals, it is more profound and pervasive than in others. But what remains true for everyone is that to diminish one's capacity to experience pain is to diminish also one's capacity to experience pleasure.

▲ ▼ ▲

In terms of operating consciously, there is an important difference between experiencing an emotion and merely naming it. Suppose, for example, I come home from work and my wife asks, "How are you feeling?" In a tense, distracted manner, I answer, "Rotten." Then my wife says sympathetically, "I can see that you're really feeling miserable." Then I allow her words to reach me, I sigh, tension begins to flow from my body, and in an altogether different tone of voice—that of a person who is no longer fighting his feelings but is owning and accepting them—I begin to tell my wife about what is troubling me. "Yes," I say to her with new authenticity, "I'm in a bad way tonight." I am now *experiencing* my emotions, not admitting and dismissing them with the dismissive word "rotten." And this is the first step toward dealing with them and moving beyond them.

In raising the level of my consciousness, I make it possible for healing to begin. Just as the body contains its own self-repairing powers, so does the mind. But these healing powers must be allowed to work. Repression obstructs the healing—meaning the *integrative*—process. One reason why people of high intelligence and great knowledge can be so helpless in the face of personal problems is that, by denying their feelings, by refusing to experience and accept them, they make it impossible for their intelligence and knowledge to go to work on the problems—to achieve the new integrations necessary to resolve them. In the example just given, by owning my feelings and dealing with my wife authentically, I connect with myself at a deeper level; I can see more clearly and think more clearly; I am no longer trapped in denial and avoidance—no longer at war with reality.

▲ ▼ ▲

If emotions are deeply repressed, obviously they must be unblocked before they can be fully experienced in the sense I am describing. In addition to the body therapies mentioned above, there are many ways in psychotherapy to facilitate the unblocking of emotion, some more effective in one context, some more effective in another. For example, there is guided fantasy, psychodrama, Gestalt techniques, journal keeping, encounter games, dream work—to name only a few widely used methods. With Ian, as we have seen, I used my "deathbed exercise." Then there are various ways of working with the organism's energy system, based on the theory of energy meridians, which facilitate not only healing but also the releasing of blocked areas from repression. Then there are the sentence completion processes that figure so prominently in my own work.

For many people, a string of sentence stems such as the following—with their corresponding completions—is quite enough to precipitate an eruption of buried feelings:

Mother (Father) was always—
With Mother (Father) I felt—
One of the things I wanted from Mother (Father) and didn't get was—
Mother (Father) gave me a view of myself as—
I can remember feeling hurt when—
I can remember feeling afraid when—
I can remember feeling angry when—
One of the things I learned to do to survive was—

Reading this list, a reader who has no experience with sentence-completion work might imagine that providing endings is very difficult. I am sometimes asked, "Suppose I don't remember?" One does not need to remember. One needs only to provide endings for each stem that will grammatically complete the sentence, *inventing* if one gets stuck, because that freedom to invent opens the door to the possibility of providing endings that are true and meaningful. I have taught this method to thousands of people. Some started out thinking they could not do it. No one still thought so fifteen minutes later. Sentence-completion work is in its very essence a consciousness-raising activity. For this reason, I have provided a lengthy appendix with a wide variety of stems to expand consciousness in different areas of life.

▲ ▼ ▲

Setting aside the technical issues in dealing with deep repression, one practice is more basic and valuable than any other in the everyday practice of living consciously, so far as our emotions are concerned. That is *the art and discipline of sustained self-observation coupled with nonjudgmental self-acceptance*. This consists of observing one's immediate state, noticing whatever is there to be noticed, without demanding that anything be different than it is—just witnessing, just being aware, without resisting or denying or disowning or condemning, breathing gently, breathing deeply—desiring nothing but to be consciously present to the immediate moment. With consistent practice, this process allows one to peel away layers of denial and disowning and to release submerged emotion.

One day, working on this book, I found myself strangely restless and distracted; the kind of effort required by writing, usually a pleasure, felt almost impossible. I got up from my computer, settled myself on the sofa in my office, closed my eyes, and focused on the feelings of restlessness moving through my body. I did not try to get rid of them: I merely watched them without judgment.

After a few minutes, the restlessness was replaced by feelings of sadness. When I felt muscles tightening to resist the sadness, I relaxed them, gently breathing a little more deeply, and allowed myself to open to the sadness with total acceptance.

For what seemed like a long time, I sat, simply experiencing the sadness.

Then the sadness began to change into tiredness, and I became aware of how tired I was of a demanding schedule that entailed the practice of psychotherapy, lectures, seminars, consulting, research, traveling—and writing a book—with inadequate time for leisure, recreation, and rejuvenation. The tiredness was mental, not physical: I was fairly conscientious about protecting myself with adequate sleep and exercise. I knew I was on this work path for a delimited period to reach particular goals—and that it was my choice to do so.

As this thought emerged, the sadness began to fade away, to be replaced by a new sense of calm. I observed this change and noted that I was curious about what might occur next.

As I went on breathing gently, I noticed that my energy level began to rise and the restlessness did not return. I felt a desire to get back to my computer and write.

This, I suddenly realized, was the kind of rest I needed, and never more so than during this period: not the rest of a vacation but of absolute stillness, such as I had been giving myself in the past few minutes. In allowing myself to feel my feelings without internally contesting them, I allowed a natural discharge to take place, and I was freed to move on, now in a more harmonious and integrated state of being.

Often the emotions we have to deal with are much more complex and difficult than in this rather simple example, but the principle is the same, as the following vignettes convey.

Claire T. was a recently divorced currency trader of thirty-nine who was struggling with a new relationship. The problem, her lover Harry L. complained, was her excessive need to control most aspects of their encounters, from the frequency of their meetings to the restaurants and movies they would attend to whom they would socialize with and when. We had reached a point in therapy where Claire was able to recognize her strong impulse to overcontrol but professed helplessness to understand the roots of this impulse.

I asked her to sit quietly and simply experience her need to control without challenging or condemning it. "Notice where in your body you feel the need, and allow yourself to own and accept it fully. No denial, no resistance, and no self-criticism, please. Just observing, just witnessing, while breathing gently and deeply, and experiencing what is there to be experienced as fully and completely as you can."

After a few minutes, tears began rolling down her cheeks. "I'm so afraid," she whispered. "Don't explain," I said. "Don't explain. Don't interrupt your process. Accept and experience the fear and allow it to lead you to whatever might come next." As she would later recount, what came next was an intensification of her fear

149

and a feeling of utter helplessness, the sense that she faced life without boundaries and could easily be invaded by any strong, forceful personality.

She sat quietly and allowed herself to witness these feelings and thoughts without speaking. Memories from childhood began to surface: memories of her father shouting at her and insisting she do things *his* way, regardless of her own preferences; memories of family members bursting into her bedroom without ever knocking; memories of her mother speaking for her when some visitor asked what she thought about something; memories of her fear to assert herself with anyone.

She looked at and experienced these memories and the feelings they evoked with no attempt at "analysis." After a while, what seemed to rise spontaneously was awareness that as an adult she had learned to fight for her sovereignty in the only way that seemed possible to her: by overcontrolling all her relationships with other people, so that to others she seemed like a fortress, while to herself she felt made of the most fragile crystal.

How she was subsequently helped to establish appropriate boundaries so that the impulse to overcontrol faded away is not part of this story; here I want to focus only on the power of nonjudgmental awareness combined with quiet acceptance.

Emotions need not be acted on when we see that to do so is counterproductive, but if they are treated with respect they can become invaluable pathways to important information, and the process of awareness and respect together often generates new integrations and actual healing. This is why so many psychotherapists stress the intrinsically curative potency of self-acceptance, and self-acceptance, of course, presupposes self-awareness. I cannot "accept" emotions ahead of experiencing them consciously; indeed, the act of experiencing them consciously is a key constituent of the acceptance process.

Marvin L., age 27, a manager of a package delivery firm, felt guilty over having engaged in malicious gossip about a fellow worker. "It's just not like me," he said. "I can't understand myself." When he told me the details of what he had done, it was obvious he expected me to reproach him or otherwise express disapproval. "I wonder where you were coming from," I said to him. "I wonder if you can get back into the feelings you had at the time and simply be with them for a time and perhaps they will begin to speak to you."

He closed his eyes and sat silently for a few minutes, sinking deeper into the memory of his emotions and observing them in the manner I had taught him. His first shock was the rage he felt against his coworker who, as he later told me, was a cheerful, self-assertive, self-confident individual—"much more so than I am." Marvin wanted to stop at this point to discuss and "analyze" his rage, but I urged him to stay with his feelings.

As he continued to observe his feelings, he noticed that the rage began to dissolve, to be replaced by humiliation and despair. And as he observed these new emotions the thought came to him that all his life he had been afraid of self-assertiveness and that he was angry at the world for his lack of courage.

Like clouds passing in the sky, this new anger, too, began to dissolve, and the realization came to him that his tendency to resent others was merely a smokescreen for his own fears and feelings of inadequacy—a misguided effort at protecting self-esteem.

At this point I encouraged him to be a witness to his sense of low self-esteem without inwardly railing against it, which was not easy for him to do. I sent him home with this assignment for the week, until our next appointment: merely to observe his unhappy feelings about himself and accept them.

"Isn't it strange," he said when we next met, "that I feel my self-esteem has risen a little this week?" I answered, "Not strange at all. When we ally ourselves with reality, self-esteem grows stronger; when we fight or deny reality, self-esteem grows weaker."

There is much more to solving our problems than merely being a witness to our thoughts and emotions, but this process is invaluable for taking us deeper into ourselves, peeling away surface layers of self-deception, and freeing the mind to address the issues that really need to be addressed.

I am thinking of a woman I treated many years ago—Clara L., then age twenty-five, a legal secretary—who came to group therapy one evening feeling nervous and depressed. A few weeks earlier, she explained, she had met a man at a party to whom she was strongly attracted and who evidently returned her feeling. After several meetings, they began an affair. The next morning, in answer to some casual question about her past life, she volunteered the information that she had once been married; the truth was that she had been married and divorced twice. It was a petty lie; she had been acutely embarrassed by it and recognized it had been prompted by a momentary fear he would lose respect for her at the knowledge she had been twice divorced at so young an age. She felt too humiliated to confess the truth. What made matters worse, she went on, was the fact that she felt happier with this man than with any other man she had known; for the first time in her life she felt visible to and appreciated by another human being. She said she could not decide what to do.

At this point, one member of the group began to lecture her on the sin of dishonesty; another interrupted to offer the warning that sooner or later the man would find out the truth anyway, so it was better to act than to face a worse predicament in the future; another suggested that her reaction of depression was exaggerated and the situation did not warrant it. Clara listened and became more and more depressed, more and more remote, and more and more helplessly bewildered.

My own conviction was that Clara had all the knowledge necessary to arrive at an appropriate decision—and that lecturing her on morality or belittling her feelings or deepening her guilt would merely aggravate her condition and solve nothing.

I therefore asked her to imagine confessing the truth to her lover, to visualize the scene as clearly as possible, and to let herself experience—and then describe aloud—her feelings of humiliation. We all waited in silence while she did so. Her eyes closed, she began the descent into her emotions, her mind empty of expectations and of any desire except the desire to be aware.

After a long while, she remarked she was experiencing the fact that she always expected to be rejected, that this was her basic orientation in important relationships.

I asked her to immerse herself as deeply as possible in her feeling of anticipated rejection—and to describe it aloud. She did so.

Then I asked her to switch her focus and immerse herself in the memory of the happiness she felt with her lover. I encouraged her to go deeper and deeper into this feeling. Again I asked that she describe aloud everything she was aware of, everything she noticed about the experience. She did so, and as she talked, the relationship became increasingly real to her emotionally. Everyone in the room could see her body relaxing, the tension leaving her, the expression on her face becoming brighter. It was clear to me that rapid integrations were taking place even as she breathed.

She suddenly opened her eyes, smiled, and said, "Oh, this is ridiculous. Of course I'm going to tell him the truth. I can't imagine what I was thinking of before."

I invited her to describe her feelings, and the first word she said was, "Happy." Then she elaborated: "As though I have more self-

153

esteem. Not just because I've decided to tell the truth. But because for the past twenty minutes I've been treating myself with respect —I mean, taking my emotions seriously—treating my emotions as *real*—not brushing myself and my feelings aside like garbage."

The technique I employed here was a variation on the pattern described above, in that I actively guided the process and, at one point, switched her focus deliberately rather than simply have her follow the flow of her feelings. But there is an underlying principle that remains the same: If we are willing to stay fully present to our emotions without denial or disowning, the result typically is not the collapse of reason but the emergence of more lucid awareness. This illustrates the precept, "Feel deeply to think clearly."

For most people, learning the art of relating to emotions in this way is not easy. Virtually everyone initially encounters difficulties. Therapy clients comment on their emotions, they "explain" their emotions, they apologize for their emotions, they speculate as to the historical origins of their emotions—and of course they *reproach* and even *ridicule* themselves for their emotions—but they find it extraordinarily difficult simply to let themselves *feel* their emotions. They have to overcome years of defenses erected to protect them against their inner life. Psychologically, self-alienation is an abnormal state, but statistically, it is normal.

▲ ▲ ▲

**If we are willing to stay fully present to our
emotions without denial or disowning, the
result typically is not the collapse of reason but
the emergence of more lucid awareness. In
other words, feel deeply to think clearly.**

▼

When the emotions with which one is struggling are unpleasant or painful, the almost universal impulse is to resist them, to convulse one's body against them—which frequently serves to intensify them. Just as the driver of a skidding car must resist the impulse to turn the wheel against the skid and instead turn the wheel into the skid to regain control, so the person hit by a disturbing emotion must learn the art of "going with" the emotion, not "against" it, to eventually dissolve or transcend it.

▲ ▼ ▲

When as adults we allow our defenses to be overcome, when we permit ourselves to experience our feelings and the memories sometimes drawn up in their wake, the result can initially be frightening. We may feel ourselves assailed by terror, pain, rage. It takes courage and discipline to stay present in such moments, resisting the temptation to shut down again and flee into unconsciousness. If we do stay present and conscious, we have the opportunity to learn and grow, but the first steps are always the hardest. It is a mark of wisdom and maturity to understand that we have the power to be a nonjudgmental witness to our emotions, thoughts, and memories without being controlled by them or driven to act in self-destructive ways.

Clearly, we need to learn impulse control. Clearly, we cannot follow emotions blindly. Our intelligence and judgment is needed to know when it is appropriate to act on our feelings. But at the same time, we should recognize that it is an error to cast reason and emotion as adversaries. What may appear as a conflict between them is in actuality a conflict between two ideas (or sets of ideas), one of which is not conscious and manifests only on the level of emotion. And it is not a foregone conclusion which idea is right. Sometimes our emotions reflect distorted perceptions and interpretations, but sometimes emotions reflect a deeper and more accurate assessment of reality. We have all, at times, acted on our conscious judgment against our feelings, and our feelings turned out to be right. We have all, at times, acted on our feelings against our conscious judgment, and our feelings turned out to be wrong. We do not follow emotions unthinkingly, but neither do we ignore or repress them. We strive to understand their meaning—to learn from them. We strive for *alignment* of thought and feeling. We strive for *integration*. But without the power of consciousness brought to our emotional life, without respectful self-observation, integration is not possible.

▲ ▲ ▲

It is a mark of wisdom and maturity to understand that we have the power to be a nonjudgmental witness to our emotions, thoughts, and memories without being controlled by them or driven to act in self-destructive ways.

▼

I recall an incident twenty-six years ago that affected me profoundly. This was during a period when I had not yet learned to be as respectful of emotions as I am today. I was out walking with the brilliant child psychologist Haim Ginott, with whom I had recently become friendly. We were discussing the relation of thought to emotion, and he remarked that most of the great mistakes he had made in life had been made when he had ignored what he was feeling. What astonished me was the sudden realization that I could have said the same about myself—I, who had on too many occasions sacrificed my emotions to what I had thought was "the reasonable." This new awareness did not lead me to ignore the voice of reason; nothing could; but it did lead me to be more careful about what I was calling "the reasonable" and to put more effort into understanding what my feelings were trying to tell me.

It is possible, however, to hold beliefs that actively obstruct this process of integration. In the effort to become more conscious, more self-aware, and to reintegrate disowned elements of one's personality, many persons are hampered by a formidable notion: the belief, mentioned above, that there are such things as "evil thoughts" and "evil emotions"—thoughts and emotions that, simply by their presence, constitute evidence of one's immorality.

Desires and emotions as such are involuntary; they are not subject to direct volitional control. The result of subconscious evaluations, they cannot be commanded in and out of existence, any more than beliefs can. But it is impossible to compute the amount of guilt and suffering produced by the notion that certain desires and emotions are proof of moral culpability. "Because I feel such-and-such, I am a rotten person." "Because I *don't* feel such-and-such, I will burn in hell."

▲ ▲ ▲

If morality means anything, it means first and foremost the commitment to be aware. Whatever forbids awareness subverts a moral existence.

▼

Self-awareness requires the freedom to approach the content of one's inner experience as a noncritical observer, an observer interested in noting facts, not in pronouncing moral judgments. This is not a counsel to abandon morality or moral judgments but to recognize their misuse in this context. To approach self-examination with the question "What does it imply about my character if I have such-and-such thoughts or such-and-such emotions?" is to make perceptual self-censorship a foregone conclusion.

If morality means anything, it means first and foremost the commitment to be aware. Whatever forbids awareness subverts a moral existence.

CONSCIOUSNESS OF OUR ACTIONS AND REACTIONS

One of the most potent sentence stems I ever developed was "If I were willing to see what I see and know what I know—" Typical endings include

I could not live the life I do.
I'd act in ways that serve me better.
I wouldn't be so self-destructive.
I'd have to face difficult choices.
I'd stop procrastinating.
I'd confront what needs to be done.
I'd have more integrity.

What the stem tends to tap into is the awareness of how often our actions do not appropriately reflect our knowledge. Sometimes our actions defy our knowledge, with unfortunate consequences.

The stem "If I bring more consciousness to my actions—" typically produces such endings as

I wouldn't make so many mistakes.
I'd accomplish more with less effort.
I wouldn't get into stupid relationships.
I'd be kinder.
I'd be more loving.
I wouldn't be so reckless.
I'd listen when my child is talking.
I wouldn't be so defensive.
My life would work better.

Sometimes, however, the endings are negative, which gives us clues as to why consciousness may be avoided:

I'd have to work harder.
People will expect more of me.
I'd realize how much I hate my job.
Suppose I made a mistake.
I couldn't claim ignorance.
I wouldn't be able to goof off.

I'd have to call some people on their mistakes, and they might
resent me.

When people choose to act without much consciousness of what
they are doing, it may be because they resist the effort of operating
consciously, because they fear what they might then be compelled
to see, or simply because it represents a change from their past
mode of operating and goes against how they see themselves. "If I
operated with more awareness," one client remarked, "I wouldn't
know myself—it wouldn't be me."

And yet, looking back on their lives, people do not regret the
times they operated consciously. They regret the times they operated unconsciously. For instance:

"If only I had let someone else drive me home that night, given what
I had been drinking."

"If only I had listened when my wife was trying to tell me."

"If only I had listened when my supervisor was trying to warn me."

"If only I had paid more attention to what our customers were
saying."

"If only I had taken seriously the messages my body was screaming
to me."

"If only my mind hadn't been wandering when I was driving
through busy traffic."

Once again I want to mention a point I made earlier: it is
context that determines the level of consciousness appropriate in
any particular situation. I need to stress this so that no one imagines I am advocating the kind of self-consciousness that paralyzes
action and causes one to trip over oneself. If, for example, I think
too much about the individual motions of my fingers while typ-

ing this on my computer, I will be less effective, not more effective. Some things are clearly best done on automatic. But an act of consciousness is required to know what those things are: to know when being on automatic is appropriate and when it is dangerous.

I can *type* on automatic, but I cannot *write* (in the sense of *create*) on automatic, even though automatic elements are involved, such as grammatical construction, and I certainly cannot *edit* on automatic—fresh consciousness is demanded.

In any event, we never want to equate "living consciously" with "living *self*-consciously," where "self-consciousness" is identified with embarrassment, inappropriate self-criticism, and the like. Living consciously means paying attention to what *needs* to be paid attention to.

▲▲▲

If I bring more consciousness to what I do
when I am angry or afraid—*I will see that*
other options exist.

▼

Among the actions and reactions we need to notice and often fail to are the things we do when we are afraid, angry, hurt, are being criticized, or are feeling drawn toward some self-destructive act. Do we tend to accept our feelings honestly or to deny or rationalize them? Do we become more conscious or less conscious? Do we try to understand or to avoid understanding? Do we try to see or to avoid seeing?

Sentence stems I've found useful include

Sometimes when I'm angry, I—
Sometimes when I'm afraid, I—
Sometimes when I'm hurt, I—

Sometimes when I'm being criticized, I—
Sometimes when I want to do something I know is bad or dangerous for me, I—

If you wrote six to ten endings for these stems every day for a
week, then studied what you had written, you would learn useful
things about yourself.

"Sometimes when I'm angry, I—" may yield such typical endings as

I say things I don't mean.
I lash out.
I look for ways to hurt.
I bottle my feelings up.
I smile.
I crack cruel jokes.
I look for who to blame.
I pretend indifference.

"Sometimes when I'm afraid, I—" may yield such typical endings as

I hide it.
I withdraw.
I start imagining catastrophe.
I feel I'm going to die.
I stop breathing.
everything inside me freezes.
I tell myself, "Don't be afraid."
I laugh nervously.
I sleep.
I take a drink.
I get angry at my husband or my children.

I can't stop talking.
I go shopping.
I sit and visualize everything terrible I can think of.

"Sometimes when I'm hurt, I—" may yield such typical endings as

I sulk.
I pretend everything is fine.
I sigh a lot.
I wait for my wife to ask, "What's wrong?" and then I answer,
    "Nothing."
I feel sorry for myself.
I expect someone to do something.
I tell myself that unhappiness is my destiny.
I think of all the times I've been hurt.
I go numb.
I bury myself in work.
I tell myself, "It's foolish to feel hurt."

"Sometimes when I'm being criticized, I—" may yield such typical endings as

I don't listen.
I get angry.
I get defensive.
I go on the offensive.
I tell myself, "I screwed up again."
I tell myself, "No one likes me."
I imagine the person is saying I'm rotten and nothing I do is any
    good, even though I know that's not what they're saying.
I apologize, even though I don't see their point.
I wish they'd stop talking.

"Sometimes when I want to do something I know is bad or dangerous for me, I—" may yield such typical endings as

I do it.

I convince myself it's OK.

I tell myself, "This time it's different."

I don't do it but I still feel miserable.

I just walk away.

I tell myself it's exciting, and next thing I know I'm doing it.

I tell myself, "I can handle things."

I say, "What's life without risk?"

I don't do it and I respect myself more.

I wonder what the temptation is, and that's all I ever do—wonder— and never come up with an answer.

I think, "Something is wrong with me" and I feel guilty, even though I don't act on the impulse.

If we want to evoke the intensified awareness that tends to stimulate change and growth (sometimes by itself, sometimes in conjunction with other therapeutic interventions), we might then shift to such sentence stems as "If I bring more consciousness to what I do when I am angry—" or "If I bring more consciousness to what I do when I am afraid—" etc.

I will cite only one of the most common and important endings one is likely to hear for these stems:

I will see that other options exist.

CONCLUDING OBSERVATIONS

Some years ago, an interesting study was done of a group of men and women who had been identified as highly creative by their peers. When this creative group was tested, it was found that the men, while in no way being unmasculine, exhibited many traits conventionally associated with femininity, such as high sensitivity, an aesthetic orientation, and so on. And the women tested, while in no way being unfeminine, were found to have many traits conventionally associated with masculinity, such as self-assertiveness, strong goal-orientation, and the like.

Early in this century, Swiss psychiatrist Carl Jung intuitively surmised that this was the case: he suggested that creative individuals tended to have a higher-than-average preponderance of traits conventionally associated with their opposite gender.

My own explanation of this phenomenon is that creative individuals tend to be more autonomous than average people and are more respectful of their inner signals. As a consequence, they tend to develop more multifaceted personalities. They do not slash away and repress whatever aspects of the self do not fit with conventional male and female stereotypes. They allow expression to a wider range of who they are. They allow themselves to hear more of their inner music. In this respect, they live more consciously, although in other areas they may not.

Accessibility to inner signals, even when they may not seem to fit any familiar model or paradigm, is one of the characteristics of creativity in particular and, more broadly, of independence—the ability to look at life through one's own eyes.

However, limiting beliefs can severely restrict this accessibility. Limiting beliefs obstruct consciousness. If, for example, I am a hardheaded businessman, scornful of the nonmaterial, who believes I could not possibly have any spiritual longings or aspirations, I may be blind to them and to the suffering caused by my denying them. If, on the other hand, my self-concept is of a nonmaterialistic seeker after ultimate truths, "above earthly concerns," I may be blind to the side of myself that hungers for some form of worldly success, if only the ability to earn a decent living, and I may not understand the "unspiritual" bitterness and resentment that sometimes assails me. In either case, my disowned self retaliates by generating a pain I cannot understand.

I once had two men with such problems in the same therapy group.

Alex K. was a thirty-eight-year-old lawyer who was contemptuous of any pursuits unrelated to money. Jim Y. was a forty-year-old psychotherapist specializing in what he called "spiritual healing." Both men were intelligent. The friction between them was often amusing. Each felt he could not stand the other and sometimes grimaced when the other was working on a problem.

Alex was unhappy because his life felt strangely empty. Jim was unhappy because each month was a struggle to pay his bills. Alex projected disdain for problems of the soul or spirit. Jim projected disdain for any form of commerce. It was obvious that they both disliked and were fascinated by each other.

There was a point toward which I was moving both men when, one day, ignoring my request that group members abstain from psychological interpretations of one another, a woman blurted out, "You're each other's disowned selves. That's why you can't stand each other. You look at each other and see the secret part of yourself you're so intent on denying."

This was the kind of identification I normally preferred that clients first name on their own, but I was obliged to admit that in this case a third person's observation struck home with both men— because in minutes, both agreed it was true. One of them said to the other, "You're like a caricature of the part of me I never wanted to know about." The other answered, "And the same back to you, brother."

The first change in each man's behavior made me smile: Alex went shopping for a book of poetry for his wife's birthday; Jim raised his therapy fees—"without guilt," he announced proudly.

A few month's later, Alex was enrolled in a course on the history of philosophy at UCLA Extension; Jim began to question the wisdom of his career choice and decided to take a year off, thinking and studying, while reflecting on what to do with the rest of his life. He made one observation that profoundly impressed me. "Alex," he remarked, "has a soul hunger for something beyond the everyday workplace. But I have a soul hunger for this world." "That means," I answered, "that what you're both in search of is balance."

As to the role of the spiritual and its relationship to living consciously, I will discuss these matters in the final chapter— "Consciousness and Spirituality."

But first, I want to address one other issue: consciousness and self-esteem.

6

Consciousness and Self-Esteem

IN this chapter, let us examine—very briefly—just a few aspects of self-esteem, and common misconceptions about it, as they pertain to the issue of living consciously.

▲ ▲ ▲

Self-esteem is the experience of being competent to cope with the basic challenges of life and of being worthy of happiness.

▼

Self-esteem is an *experience*. It is a particular way of *experiencing* the self. It is a good deal more than a mere feeling—this must be stressed. It involves emotional, evaluative, and cognitive components. It also entails certain *action dispositions:* to move toward life rather than away from it; to move toward consciousness rather than away from it; to treat facts with respect rather than denial; to operate self-responsibly rather than the opposite.

To begin with a definition: *Self-esteem is the disposition to experi-*

ence oneself as being competent to cope with the basic challenges of life and as being worthy of happiness.[1] It is confidence in the efficacy of our mind, in our ability to think. By extension, it is confidence in our ability to learn, make appropriate choices and decisions, and respond effectively to change. It is also the experience that success, achievement, fulfillment—*happiness*—are right and natural for us. The survival value of such confidence is obvious; so is the danger when it is missing.

Self-esteem is not the euphoria or buoyancy that may be temporarily induced by a drug, a compliment, or a love affair. It is not an illusion or hallucination. If it is not grounded in reality, if it is not built over time through the appropriate operation of mind, it is not self-esteem.[2]

The root of our need for self-esteem is the need for a consciousness to learn to trust itself. And the root of the need to learn such trust is the fact that consciousness is volitional, as we saw in chapter 2. We control the switch that turns consciousness brighter or dimmer. We are not rational—that is, reality-focused—*automatically.* This means that whether we learn to operate our mind in such a way as to make ourselves *appropriate to life* is ultimately a function of our choices. Do we strive for consciousness or for its opposite? For rationality or its opposite? For coherence and clarity or their opposite? For truth or its opposite? All the other self-esteem virtues, about which I write in *The Six Pillars of Self-Esteem* —self-acceptance, self-responsibility, self-assertiveness, purposefulness, integrity—rest on the foundation of a pro-consciousness orientation and are not possible without it.

"Living consciously" is the first of the "six pillars." To clarify why it is the necessary base of all the others, I will state their essence:

The practice of self-acceptance: the willingness to own, experience, and take responsibility for our thoughts, feelings, and actions, without evasion, denial, or disowning—and also without self-repudiation; giving oneself permission to think one's thoughts, experience one's emotions, and look at one's actions without necessarily liking, endorsing, or condoning them; the virtue of realism applied to the self.

The practice of self-responsibility: realizing that we are the author of our choices and actions; that each one of us is responsible for our life and well-being and for the attainment of our goals; that if we need the cooperation of other people to achieve our goals, we must offer values in exchange; and that the question is not "Who's to blame?" but always "What needs to be done?" ("What do *I* need to do?")

The practice of self-assertiveness: being authentic in our dealings with others; treating our values and persons with decent respect in social contexts; refusing to fake the reality of who we are or what we esteem in order to avoid disapproval; the willingness to stand up for ourselves and our ideas in appropriate ways in appropriate contexts.

The practice of living purposefully: identifying our short-term and long-term goals or purposes and the actions needed to attain them (formulating an action plan); organizing behavior in the service of those goals; monitoring action to be sure we stay on track; and paying attention to outcome so as to recognize if and when we need to go back to the drawing board.

The practice of personal integrity: living with congruence between what we know, what we profess, and what we do; telling the truth, honoring our commitments, exemplifying in action the values we profess to admire.

What all these practices have in common is respect for reality, which is the essence of living consciously. They all entail at their core a set of *mental operations* (which, naturally, have consequences in the external world).

When we seek to align ourselves with reality as best we understand it, we nurture and support our self-esteem. When, either out of fear or desire, we seek escape from reality, we undermine our self-esteem. No other issue is more important or basic than our cognitive relationship to reality—meaning, to that which exists.

A consciousness cannot trust itself if in the face of discomfiting facts it has a policy of preferring blindness to sight. A person cannot experience self-respect who too often in action betrays consciousness, knowledge, and conviction—that is, who operates without integrity.

Thus, if we are mindful in this area we see that self-esteem is not a free gift of nature. It has to be cultivated—has to be earned. It cannot be acquired by blowing oneself a kiss in the mirror and saying, "Good morning, Perfect." It cannot be attained by being showered with praise. Nor by sexual conquests. Nor by material acquisitions. Nor by a hypnotist planting the thought that one is wonderful. Nor by allowing young people to believe they are better students than they really are and know more than they really know; faking reality is not a path to mental health or authentic self-assurance. However, just as people dream of attaining effortless wealth, so they dream of attaining effortless self-esteem —and unfortunately, the marketplace is full of panderers to this longing. (And this makes it very easy for critics of the whole idea of self-esteem to find ready targets for their ridicule.)

People can be inspired, stimulated, or coached to live more consciously, practice greater self-acceptance, operate more self-responsibly, function more self-assertively, live more purposefully, and bring a higher level of personal integrity into their lives—but the task of generating and sustaining these practices falls on each of us alone. "If I bring a higher level of awareness to my self-esteem, I see that mine is the responsibility of nurturing it." No one—not our parents nor our friends nor our lover nor our psychotherapist nor our support group—can "give" us self-esteem. If and when we fully grasp this, *that* is an act of "waking up." In the spring of 1993, a famous feminist addressed the National Council for Self-Esteem and, confronting the question of how one could best raise one's self-esteem, volunteered as her *first* suggestion: "Join a support group"—thereby encouraging the notion that the source of self-esteem is external. It is this very belief that causes no end of suffering to people who look for the source of self-esteem everywhere but within. A woman in the audience later remarked to me, "All my support group ever did was encourage me to see myself as a victim—just the opposite of what I needed if I was to learn to take responsibility for myself." Perhaps I should mention that I am not opposed to support groups per se; some can be very helpful, depending on their basic philosophy; what I challenge is placing membership in a support group at the top of one's list of recommendations for growing in self-esteem.

MISCONCEPTIONS ABOUT SELF-ESTEEM

When we do not understand the principles suggested above, we tend to seek self-esteem where it cannot be found—and, if we are in "the self-esteem movement," to communicate our misunderstandings to others.

Teachers who embrace the idea that self-esteem is important without adequately grasping its roots may announce (to quote one such teacher) that "self-esteem comes primarily from one's peers." Or (quoting many others): "Children should not be graded for mastery of a subject, because it will be hurtful to their self-esteem." Or (quoting still others): "Self-esteem is best nurtured by selfless (!) service to the community."

▲▲▲

**The root of our self-esteem is not our
achievements per se but those internally
generated practices that make it possible for us
to achieve.**

▼

In the "recovery movement" and from so-called spiritual leaders in general one may receive a different message: "Stop struggling to achieve self-esteem. Turn your problems over to God. Realize that you are a child of God—and that is all you need to have self-esteem." Consider what this implies if taken literally. We don't need to live consciously. We don't need to act self-responsibly. We don't need to have integrity. All we have to do is surrender responsibility to God, and effortless self-esteem is guaranteed to us. This is not a helpful message to convey to people. Nor is it true.

Yet another misconception—very different from those I have just discussed—is the belief that the measure of our personal worth is our external achievements. This is an understandable error to make, but it is an error nonetheless. We admire achievements, in ourselves and in others, and it is natural and appropriate to do so. But this is not the same thing as saying that our achievements are the measure or grounds of our self-esteem. The root of our self-esteem is not our achievements per se but those internally generated practices that make it possible for us to achieve. How much we will achieve in the world is not fully in our control. An economic depression can temporarily put us out of work. A depression cannot take away the resourcefulness that will allow us sooner or later to find another job or to go into business for ourselves. "Resourcefulness" is not an achievement in the world (although it may result in that); it is an action in consciousness— and it is here that self-esteem is generated.

To clarify further the importance of understanding what self-esteem is and is not, and how it relates to living consciously, I want to comment on a recent research report that has gained a great deal of attention in the media and has been used to challenge the value of self-esteem.

By way of preamble, let me say that one of the most depressing aspects of so many discussions of self-esteem today is the absence of any reference to the importance of thinking or respect for reality. Too often, consciousness and rationality are not judged to be relevant, since they are not raised as considerations. The notion seems to be that *any* positive feeling about the self, however arrived at and regardless of its grounds, equals "self-esteem."

We encounter this assumption in a much-publicized research paper by Roy F. Baumeister, Joseph M. Boden, and Laura Smart, entitled "Relation of Threatened Egotism to Violence and Aggression: The Dark Side of High Self-Esteem." In it, the authors write:

> *Conventional wisdom has regarded low self-esteem as an important cause of violence, but the opposite view is theoretically viable. An interdisciplinary review of evidence about aggression, crime, and violence contradicted the view that low self-esteem is an important cause. Instead, violence appears to be most commonly a result of threatened egotism—that is, highly favorable views of self that are disputed by some person or circumstance. Inflated, unstable, or tentative beliefs in the self's superiority may be most prone to encountering threats and hence to causing violence. The mediating process may involve directing anger outward as a way of avoiding a downward revision of the self-concept.[3]*

The article contains more astonishing statements than it is possible to quote, but here are a few representative examples:

"In our view, the benefits of favorable self-opinions accrue primarily to the self, and they are if anything a burden and potential problem to everyone else." "By *self-esteem* we mean simply a favorable global evaluation of oneself. The term *self-esteem* has acquired highly positive connotations, but it has simple synonyms the connotations of which are more mixed, including . . . egotism, arrogance . . . conceitedness, narcissism, and sense of superiority, which share the fundamental meaning of favorable self-evaluation." "[W]e propose that the major cause of violence is high self-esteem combined with an ego threat [which is caused by someone challenging your self-evaluation]." "Apparently, then, alcohol generally helps create a state of high self-esteem."

Observe, first of all, that nothing in the authors' idea of self-esteem would allow one to distinguish between an individual whose self-esteem is rooted in the practices of living consciously, self-responsibility, and personal integrity—that is, one whose self-esteem is rooted *in reality*—and one whose "self-esteem" consists of grandiosity, fantasies of superiority, exaggerated notions of one's accomplishments, megalomania, and "favorable global self-evaluations" induced by drugs and alcohol. No definition of self-esteem or piece of research that obliterates a distinction of this fundamentality can make any claim to scientific legitimacy. It leaves *reality* out of its analysis.

One does not need to be a trained psychologist to know that some people with low self-esteem strive to compensate for their deficit by boasting, arrogance, and conceited behavior. What educated person does not know about compensatory defense mechanisms? One has to be very deeply committed to unconsciousness to see self-esteem manifested in the neurosis we call narcissism—or in megalomania. One has to be no less committed to unconsciousness to equate in self-esteem the trailblazing scientist or entrepreneur, moved by intellectual self-trust and a passion to discover or achieve, and the terrorist who must sustain his "high self-evaluation" with periodic fixes of torture and murder. To offer both types as instances of "high self-esteem" is to empty the term of any usable meaning.

An important purpose of fresh thinking is to provide us with new and valuable distinctions that will allow us to navigate more effectively through reality. What is the purpose of "thinking" that destroys distinctions already known to us that are of life-and-death importance?

It is tempting to comment on this report in greater detail, because it contains so many instances of specious reasoning. However, such a discussion would not be relevant here, since my intention is only to show the importance of a precise understanding of self-esteem and also to show what can happen when consciousness and reality are omitted from the investigation.

So I will conclude with one last observation. In an interview given to a journalist, one of the researchers (Roy F. Baumeister), explaining his opposition to the goal of raising people's self-esteem, is quoted as saying: "Ask yourself: If everybody were 50 percent more conceited, would the world be a better place?"[4] The implication is clearly that self-esteem and conceit are the same thing—both undesirable. *Webster's New World Dictionary* defines conceit as "an exaggerated opinion of oneself, one's merits, etc." No, the world would not be a better place if everybody were 50 percent more conceited. But would the world be a better place if everybody had *earned* a 50 percent higher level of self-esteem, by living consciously, responsibly, and with integrity? Yes, it would—enormously.

AWARENESS OF WHAT AFFECTS OUR SELF-ESTEEM

Self-esteem reflects our deepest vision of our competence and worth. Sometimes this vision is our most closely guarded secret, even from ourselves, as when we try to compensate for our deficiencies with what I call *pseudo*-self-esteem—a pretense at a self-confidence and self-respect we do not actually feel. Nothing is more common than the effort to protect self-esteem not with consciousness but with unconsciousness—with denial and evasion—which only results in a further deterioration of self-esteem. Indeed, a good deal of the behavior we call "neurotic" can best be understood as a misguided effort to protect self-esteem by means that in fact are undermining.

▲ ▲ ▲

**Self-esteem reflects our deepest vision of our
competence and worth.**

▼

Whether or not we admit it, there is a level at which all of us know that the issue of our self-esteem is of the most burning importance. Evidence for this observation is the defensiveness with which insecure people may respond when their errors are pointed out. Or the extraordinary feats of avoidance and self-deception people can exhibit with regard to gross acts of unconsciousness and irresponsibility. Or the foolish and pathetic ways people some-times try to prop up their egos by the wealth or prestige of their spouse, the make of their automobile, the fame of their dress designer, or the exclusiveness of their golf club. In more recent times, as the subject of self-esteem has gained increasing attention, one way of masking one's problems in this area is with the angry denial that self-esteem is a value.

Not all the values with which people may attempt to support a pseudo-self-esteem are foolish or irrational. Productive work, for instance, is certainly a value to be admired, but if one tries to compensate for deficient self-esteem by becoming a workaholic, one is in a battle one can never win—nothing will ever feel like "enough." Kindness and compassion are undeniably virtues and they are part of what it means to lead a moral life, but they are no substitutes for consciousness, independence, self-responsibility, and integrity. People who do not understand this often use kindness and compassion as disguised means to buy "love" and perhaps even a sense of moral superiority: "I'm more kind and compassion-ate than you'll ever be, and if I weren't so humble, I'd tell you so."

▲ ▲ ▲

**In the world of the future, children will be
taught the basic dynamics of self-esteem and
the power of living consciously and
self-responsibly.**

▼

One of the great challenges to our practice of living consciously is to pay attention to what *in fact* nurtures our self-esteem or deteriorates it. The reality may be very different from our beliefs. We may, for example, get a very pleasant "hit" from someone's compliment, and we may tell ourselves that when we win people's approval we have self-esteem, but then, if we are adequately con-scious, we may notice that the pleasant feeling fades rather quickly and that we seem to be insatiable and never fully satisfied. This may direct us to wonder if we have thought deeply enough about the sources of genuine self-approval. Or we may notice that when we give our conscientious best to a task, face a difficult truth with courage, take responsibility for our actions, speak up when we know that is what the situation warrants, refuse to betray our convictions, or persevere even when persevering is not easy—our self-esteem rises. We may also notice that if and when we do the opposite, self-esteem falls. But of course, all such observations imply that we have chosen to be conscious.

In the world of the future, children will be taught the basic dynamics of self-esteem and the power of living consciously and self-responsibly. They will be taught what self-esteem is, why it is important, and what it depends on. They will learn to distinguish between authentic self-esteem and pseudo-self-esteem. They will be guided to acquire this knowledge because it will have become apparent to virtually everyone that the ability to think (and to learn and to respond confidently to change) is our basic means of survival—and that it cannot be faked. The purpose of school is to prepare young people for the challenges of adult life. They will need this understanding to be adaptive to an information age in which self-esteem has acquired such urgency. In a fiercely competitive global economy—with every kind of change happening faster and faster—there is little market for unconsciousness, passivity, or self-doubt. In the language of business, low self-esteem—underdeveloped mindfulness—puts one at a competitive disadvantage. However, neither teachers in general nor teachers of self-esteem in particular can do their jobs properly—or communicate the importance of their work—until they themselves understand the intimate linkage that exists between living consciously, self-esteem, and appropriate adaptation to reality. "The world of the future" begins with this understanding.

7

Consciousness and Spirituality

IN today's cultural context, I have noticed that if I raise with lecture audiences the issue of living consciously, certain questions almost invariably arise:

What is the relationship, if any, between living consciously and pursuing a spiritual path?

If there is a connection between living consciously and spirituality, where and how does a belief in God fit into the picture—or does it?

What is the relation, if any, between living consciously, spirituality, and the teachings of mysticism?

In addressing these questions, we will be led into a discussion somewhat more technical and abstract than was necessary in most of the preceding chapters. However, at a time in history when more and more people in the West seem to be thinking with a new sense of urgency about issues such as consciousness, spirituality, and mysticism, I believe this exploration can be of value. The final subject to which we are led may be of particular interest to many readers: the ethics of mysticism examined through the lens of reason.

In chapter 1, we considered the nature of reason. In this chapter, we are going to look at some of the beliefs of those who claim to have gone "beyond reason."

First, what *is* spirituality?

DEFINITIONS: THE IMPORTANCE
OF BEING CLEAR ABOUT MEANINGS

Many years ago, reflecting on the question of what precisely spirituality means, I telephoned one of the most brilliant men I know (our disagreements notwithstanding)—Ken Wilber, famous for the profundity of his writings concerning the world's spiritual traditions and their relation to Western psychology. I asked him, "Could you provide me with a good definition of what precisely you mean by 'spiritual'?" After a moment of silence he chuckled and answered, "Not really."

And here we encounter the first of many difficulties in examining issues in this sphere—the absence of clear definitions of what any writer or speaker means. Actually, the problem may be worse than that: often there does not seem to be any perceived need for clear definitions. Not uncommonly the attitude projected is: "Oh, you know what I mean by 'spiritual.'" Or: "You know what I mean by 'God.'" Or: "You know what I mean by—" fill in your favorite mystical term. The truth is, it is very easy for people to talk at length about great issues without any clear idea of what in reality their key terms denote.

The word "spirit," in its origins, means "breath." Spirit pertained to the breath of life. When Aristotle spoke about spirit (or soul), he meant that by virtue of which an organism is alive. To this day, when we speak of a person or a horse as "high spirited," we mean full of life. Or when we speak of a person's spirit being broken, we mean that the person's will to live self-assertively has been extinguished—the life force has been subdued. So on this understanding, "spiritual" would mean pertaining to the life force or the life principle. However, this is not the primary meaning the term has for most of us today, although it is how many dictionaries still define it.

Long ago, many people shifted the focus from *life* to *consciousness* (or soul) as the central component of spirituality. "Spirit" now denotes something closer to "the life force or life principle as manifest in consciousness." That is how I think of the term. And "spirituality" is best understood as meaning *pertaining to consciousness and to the needs and development of consciousness.* (The connection to the earlier meaning lies in the fact that consciousness is usually understood to be an attribute of life at a certain level of organization.) One advantage of this definition is that it is neutral: It does not commit one to any specific position concerning what a spiritual life might consist of, nor does it commit one to any particular religious belief.

Further, note that we usually mean "spiritual" to be contrasted with "material" and "materialistic." Those who use the term "spiritual" in today's context almost invariably hold, as I do, that spirit or consciousness is nonmaterial—not constituted of matter. When we call a person "materialistic," we usually mean he or she is overly concerned with the material and short-term (and with physical gratification devoid of deeper significance). In contrast, a "spiritual" person is one who is concerned with the needs and development of consciousness and with the timeless and enduring (with no necessary implication of contempt for the physical, temporal, secular, or of any spirit/body dichotomy).

Such, at any rate, is how I intend the words to be understood in this discussion.

SPIRITUALITY: A THIS-WORLDLY INTERPRETATION

▲ ▲ ▲

**Whoever continually strives to achieve a
clearer and clearer vision of reality and our
place in it—whoever is pulled forward by a
passion for such clarity—is, to that extent,
leading a spiritual life.**

▼

If *spirituality* means pertaining to consciousness and the needs and development of consciousness, then whoever commits to awareness and personal growth as a way of life—which entails, among other things, self-awareness and self-examination—is on a spiritual path.

When I wrote *The Six Pillars of Self-Esteem,* I was aware I was presenting a spiritual discipline, although I did not name it as such. To train oneself in the six pillars as a consistent practice, to seek to integrate them into one's daily life and activities—so that they become a way of being—is to be dedicated to spiritual development.

Whoever continually strives to achieve a clearer and clearer vision of reality and his or her place in it—whoever is pulled forward by a *passion* for such clarity—is, to that extent, leading a spiritual life.

The rest is a matter of degree, measured by the amount of time one invests and the intensity of one's involvement.

It is often observed that spirituality is primarily the domain of *experience,* of a person's direct relation with reality. Religion is primarily the domain of *beliefs, rules,* and *rituals.* Authentic spirituality is reflected in how one lives and how one experiences existence, not in what one professes to believe; it is intrinsically individualistic rather than conformist. A person may use his or her religion to inspire a personal spiritual journey, a quest for

181

greater consciousness, but religion itself does not necessarily imply any such quest. Indeed, it may support the *illusion* of spirituality while leading in the opposite direction—by demanding that consciousness be sacrificed to faith and threatening hell as punishment for thinking, or by ridiculing a person's struggle to make sense out of what is being taught. So, about any tenet one must ask: Does this support or constrict the active use of my mind? Is this teaching addressed to my understanding or to my fears? Am I being offered awareness or escape from the responsibility of awareness? The courage to raise and confront such questions is itself a spiritual achievement. It is consciousness committed to its own growth and self-actualization.

It is easy enough to believe that if one goes to church on Sunday, listens to a sermon, and sings a few hymns, one's life has a spiritual center. However, such a practice may be the opposite of what we imagine it to be: it may arrest the mind in a complacent contemplation of the comfortably accepted, the beliefs with which one was raised. Spirit—in contrast—is a summons to rise, to shatter and transcend the boundaries of the familiar.

Consciousness has been evolving and developing since our first emergence on this planet. Just as in the life of a single human being we grow from the primitive mode of awareness of an infant to progressively more advanced and powerful forms of consciousness—ultimately learning to grasp and work with the most complex principles and abstractions, not only able to think but *to think about thinking*—that is, mind examining itself and its operations—so, as a species, over thousands of years, we have gone through this same course of development. Reason, as we understand the process today, is the product of an enormous span of evolutionary time.

And even today, those who operate at reason's higher levels are a small minority of the human race. While the capacity for this level of functioning begins to emerge in early adolescence, unless it is developed, actualized, and sustained, it tends to be lost as a possibility for most adults. (This was the conclusion of Jean Piaget, our foremost student of cognitive development.) In any event, it hardly needs to be argued that the level of mental operations of the average person is suboptimal. Most people do not remotely approach the potential of mind, neither the potential as we now know it nor the potential as we may yet only suspect it.

▲▲▲

**Evolution continues in us and through us, and
our developmental possibilities are almost
beyond speculation.**

▼

By this last phrase I wish to draw attention to the fact that there are no grounds for assuming the course of evolution has stopped. Evolution continues in us and through us, and our developmental possibilities are almost beyond speculation. The ability of certain individuals to control physiological processes ordinarily assumed to be involuntary is only a simple and fairly primitive example of what I mean. At every stage of our evolution, individuals have exhibited capacities not shared by most others at the time but that became common later in our history. For example, during a period when most humans' mental operations were still overwhelmingly sense-bound, some persons, already more evolved, manifested a capacity for abstract, logical reflection; they were the forerunners of humanity's future.

Very likely some of those whose cognitive level was more primitive looked on those whose capacities were more developed as possessing "supernatural" powers. "Supernatural" is often the name we give to that which is outside the range of what we believe is possible. But of course, with the progress of knowledge, humans came to recognize that abstract thought is as "natural" as sensory perception. Similarly, today, we sometimes call "irrational" or "mystical" that which does not fit our model of the world or our ideas about what is "reasonable"—a mistake pointed out in chapter 1. As we shall see, "mysticism" has a very specific meaning, and we only confuse ourselves if we fling the term about in inappropriate ways.

Any number of spiritual disciplines—Western and Eastern—present themselves as aiming at the evolutionary development of consciousness and as offering a vision of reality superior to the world as perceived by a mind looking through the filters of tradition, culture, and personal neurosis. One of the evidences of their growing influence is that more and more Westerners are exploring the practice of meditation and are discovering its multiple benefits —as a path to self-understanding, enhanced creativity, a deeper appreciation of what is important in life, a clearer grasp of one's own mental processes, a more profound perception of reality, and the experience of greater serenity. All this is quite apart from the issue of whether or not one subscribes to the religious or philosophical presuppositions of any particular meditative practice. Many enthusiastic meditators have little or no personal interest in religion or mysticism. There is nothing "mystical" about meditation per se.

Unsurprisingly, the results of meditation vary enormously from individual to individual. For one person, meditation is a helpful means to enhanced relaxation; for another, an invaluable tool for self-understanding; for another, a source of spiritual transformation and growth. No doubt the outcome for a given individual is determined by a number of factors, including one's initial motivation and overall psychological state, the kind of meditation one practices, and the quality of one's teacher, to name only three.

For a great many persons, pursuit of a spiritual path does entail not merely meditative practice but immersion in one or another spiritual or religious or mystical discipline. In challenging some fundamental claims of these disciplines, I am not concerned with the practice of meditation, in which I see great value, but with the religious or metaphysical conclusions at which these disciples claim to have arrived—and with the epistemology of mysticism itself; that is, with how its claims to knowledge are justified. The reason

I feel obliged briefly to discuss mysticism here is because of the linkage that exists in many people's minds between consciousness, spirituality, and Western or Eastern "wisdom traditions."

But there is some ground I need to clear first.

GOD: AN ALL-PURPOSE WORD REFERRING TO—?

For many people, the term "spiritual" has a meaning quite different from the one I have discussed. The evolution of consciousness or mind is no part of what they are thinking of. For them, "spirituality" means—and only means—a deep preoccupation with knowing and loving God (however this term is interpreted). If they think of "the needs and development of consciousness," it is only with regard to this concern.

One of the difficulties with their definition lies in what it cannot accommodate. No one will deny that Buddhism is one of the word's great spiritual disciplines or religions. And yet in original Buddhism there is no mention of any God.[1] (Nor is there in the Japanese religion of Shinto.) Its opponents reviled Buddhism as atheistic. Or again, today most people would agree that the Dalai Lama—a Tibetan Buddhist—is an impressive spiritual leader. And yet, when asked in an interview why he did not talk about God, he replied that in his observation, people no more benefited their soul's development by preoccupying themselves with God than by obsessing about material acquisitions. One does not have to share all the conclusions of Buddhism to concede that Buddhists are concerned with the needs and development of consciousness. Indeed, they have studied consciousness and its workings far more than any Western religion. (However, there has always been an anti-conceptual thread running through most mystical schools, including Buddhism. St. Thomas Aquinas, the greatest philosopher of the Middle Ages and the man who reintroduced Aristotle to Western culture, was superior in his understanding and treatment of the human conceptual faculty and our unique reasoning abilities.) So to narrow our understanding of spirituality to a concern with God—or even a belief in God—is unjustifiably restrictive. One could say that such a view is metaphysically parochial.

▲▼▲

I have long been interested in the relation between professed beliefs and behavior. And through many years of experience, I have noticed that I cannot predict a single action merely from knowing that a person claims to believe or not to believe in God. The only exception is that if a person professes belief in God, there is a higher probability that he or she will go to church and engage in prayer. But as to how productive a person will be, how fair, just, and benevolent in human dealings, how open or closed to rational discussion—I have never been able to predict *any* of this if all I have to go on is the statement "I do—or do not—believe in God." I have known kind and benevolent theists and kind and benevolent atheists—and, of course, I have also known the opposite. I have known highly creative theists and highly creative atheists—and the opposite. I have known theists who lived focused and rational lives and atheists who did likewise—and the opposite.

Theoretically, one would imagine that which belief a person held would show up in significant traits and behaviors—such as productivity, ambition, sense of justice, personal integrity, basic decency, inner serenity, resourcefulness in coping with adversity, or ability to enjoy life. When I was a young man, I felt certain that such opposing perspectives must produce gross differences in these areas. I felt there *should* be differences. But I have never found any evidence or seen any research to support my feeling.

Let me stress that I am not talking about whether or not a person describes him- or herself as "religious." That is a different question. Here I am referring only to the presence or absence of an expressed belief in God. And my point is that that belief (or absence of belief), per se, tells us nothing about a person's spiritual, ethical, or psychological development.

One explanation is that people mean vastly different things by the term "God," and it is a great mistake to dismiss those differences as unimportant. It is a cliché to assert that "we all worship the same God," but it is not true. Even between the Jewish God and the Christian God there are differences, if one takes seriously the Christian idea of the Trinity. But even if Jews and Christians (and Muslims) can talk about "our heavenly father" with some significant congruence of meaning, what of the Deist who thinks of God as an Impersonal Force or Intelligence that started the universe off but has since retired from the scene, no longer participating in human affairs? And what will we say about the mystic who speaks of God as "the Suchness of Things"? Are they *in any meaningful sense* all talking about the same entity? I do not think so.

If we do not know what a person *means* by "God," we know almost nothing about the significance of a professed belief. And if we think the idea of God is at least worthy of intellectual consideration, we do not shrug off radical differences of definition as trivial and do not blithely assert that "we all worship the same God."

Unfortunately, most people can explain what they mean by "God" only in hopelessly vague terms—by use of metaphors, symbolism, floating abstractions, or by talking only about what God is *not.* "God" is not a term given a precise, intelligible meaning, not even by theologians. Indeed, by the criteria we apply to other terms, it is not meaningful at all.[2] And if this is so, then debating about God's existence or nonexistence is a dubious exercise.

In addition, there is the issue of what role "God" plays in a believer's life. For some, "God" is merely an intellectual construct that does not affect them in any significant way. For others, a continuing source of comfort. For others, a source of reproach and terror. For others, a cause to believe that *someone* in the universe loves them. For others, a justification for the consoling idea that everything happens for a reason and that seeming tragedies have a higher purpose. For others, the ultimate spiritual context that holds the total of their existence.

▲ ▼ ▲

I remember as a boy trying to make sense of the idea of God. I was always wanting to understand what people mean by the term. Belief "on faith" was anathema to me. I wanted to *understand*. I recall being troubled, around the age of ten, by the notion that "God is everywhere." How could an entity be *everywhere?* The only solution I could produce was the thought that God could be *everywhere* only if he were *everything*. In effect, I came up with the idea of a primitive pantheism—and for a few weeks felt quite proud of my ingenuity. I concluded that I knew what people "really meant," even if they did not know it themselves. But then I was stopped by the realization that if "God" and "Everything" (or "the Universe" or "Nature") all meant the same thing, all referred to the same reality, throwing in the term "God" added nothing to my understanding. I began to suspect that using "God" in this way represented an attempt to salvage the term while making the idea superfluous.

I pestered many people—family members, friends, parents of friends, teachers, Jews, Protestants, Catholics—with two questions: "What do you *mean* by 'God'?" And "Why do you assert his existence?" A rabbi answered, "I mean by 'God' the creator of the universe, and I believe in him because how else can you explain that we are all here or that the universe even exists?" I felt there was some flaw in what the rabbi was saying, but I could not answer him in that moment.

▲ ▲ ▲

The universe *is*. This is where we must begin.

▼

I became an atheist at the age of twelve when one day, walking down my street and reflecting on the rabbi's words, I looked up at the sky and had an electrifying experience. In retrospect, I would call it a *spiritual* experience. I was hit by a sudden sense of the universe as a total, in all its unimaginable immensity, and I thought: if God is needed to explain the existence of the universe, then what explains the existence of God? After all, if God does exist, he's at least as marvelous and impressive as the universe, *and therefore no less in need of an explanation.* But then who or what created God? And then who or what created whatever created God? We're stuck with an infinite regress. But if that's no good and we have to begin *somewhere,* isn't it more reasonable to accept the existence of the universe—of *being,* whatever its form—as the starting point of everything? (Begin with existence itself, I would later learn to say, as the ultimate, irreducible primary.) Whatever stages of development the universe may go through, whatever its form at different points in time, in an ultimate sense, *the universe is.* This is where we must begin. I felt a great rush of exhilaration and, looking at the blue sky overhead, at the green of the trees on our block, at people sitting on porches, automobiles passing by, and children playing on the sidewalk, I felt a love of a kind I had never experienced before: a love for being. A love for existence itself. I felt a great sense of serenity.

"The smartest men believe in God!" my mother yelled at me that night at dinner. *"Einstein* believes in God! How can you not believe in God?"

I countered, "But *why* do people believe?"

"They're brilliant men. They must know."

I heard versions of that argument many times. At school someone said, "Do you think you're the only one who knows what's true—and everyone else is wrong?" I began to suspect that most people believed in God only because others did, rather than because of any perceptions, knowledge, or experience of their own. I wondered if this might be the ground for many of their beliefs, a theme I would explore years later in *Taking Responsibility,* in my discussion of social metaphysics.[3]

Over the centuries, philosophers have attempted to develop rational proofs for the existence of God (however defined), in order to demonstrate that theism does not necessarily require an act of faith or a mystical experience. All such attempts have failed.[4] Time and time again other philosophers have shown that the arguments do not hold; not one of them has been immune to refutation. (However, if a particular individual is persuaded by one of these arguments, not knowing how to refute it, then his or her acceptance of theism is not blind faith.) It is important to observe that many believers object even to the *attempt* to ground a belief in God in reason. They feel that a God whose existence one can *prove* is no God at all—merely a scientific phenomenon. Their attitude is: if reason cannot accommodate God, so much the better for God and so much the worse for reason—meaning the problem is reason's, not God's.

▲ ▲ ▲

Living consciously insists on asking, What are
the *grounds* of your belief? What is the
evidence?

▼

My purpose here is not to argue for or against the existence of God. That would require a much longer discussion and the examination of many more issues. And while I personally have never heard an argument nor had an experience that would make the idea of God (however defined) at all plausible to me, this is not a subject about which I am militant.

My purpose here is twofold: First, to separate a belief in God from any part of what *I* mean by living consciously, and second, to point out that if we understand reason as I have defined it in chapter 1, we must realize that in declaring "So much the worse for reason," we are declaring, "So much the worse for consciousness." It is not an expression of living consciously to say, "I feel it, therefore it's true." Living consciously insists on asking, What are the *grounds* of your belief? What is the *evidence?*

Just as we must challenge the error of identifying spirituality with theism or religion and assuming that they are intrinsically or necessarily related, so we must challenge other common assumptions about spirituality, no less erroneous. They are the identification of spirituality with self-transcendence,

mysticism,

an ethics of selflessness.

Let us consider each of these issues in turn.

SELF-TRANSCENDENCE: BUT WHO IS DOING THE TRANSCENDING?

In spiritual literature, the idea of "self-transcendence" often figures prominently. It is often coupled with "the dissolution of ego." The premise is that the evolution of consciousness inevitably leads to the realization that *self* is a prison to be escaped.

Buddhism, which has become increasingly popular and influential in the West, capturing the enthusiasm of many who see themselves as being on a spiritual path, goes still further. It asserts that the *self* does not exist—it is only an illusion—and "waking up" entails letting go of this illusion. Buddhism teaches that the prison from which one must escape is not *self* but the belief that one is or has a self. It proposes meditative self-observation—sustained observation of one's inner processes—as a means to the achievement of this liberation. As a Buddhist scholar expressed it to me, "Self-observation facilitates self-transcendence. The notion of personal identity is discarded." The question that immediately arises is: If and when the gates of enlightenment finally open, *who will walk through,* now that self, ego, and identity are gone?

▲▲▲

Who is transcending? The answer is: *I* am.
From this simple and obvious truth, there can
be no escape.

▼

To *transcend* is to rise above a limited context or perspective to a wider field of vision. The wider field of vision does not negate

191

or deny the previous, narrower field, but includes and goes beyond it. As I discussed in *Honoring the Self,* growth itself can be seen as a series of transcendences, as we move from one stage of development to a higher one, emotionally, cognitively, morally, and so forth. Thus, for example, according to Piaget's theory of stages of cognitive development, we transcend one level of mental operation to reach a higher level.[5] Similarly, with Kohlberg's theory of stages of moral development, we transcend one level of moral perspective to reach a higher one.[6] In a different sense but reflecting the same principle, when we outgrow dependence to the extent that we leave family and learn to exist as self-supporting individuals, we transcend one level of development to attain a higher one—we are moving toward autonomy. And ideally, when I cease to identify exclusively with my body, my emotions, my beliefs, or my thoughts, when I realize that my ultimate "I"—my *ego*—is the unifying center of awareness itself (that which thinks, chooses, wills) and not the *contents* of awareness, I am shifting from a lower vision of self-in-the-world to a higher and more mature one. And this, I submit, is what transcendence *always* means when used in its legitimate sense.

To come to the heart of the issue we must now ask: *Who* is transcending? The answer is: *I* am. From this simple and obvious truth, there can be no escape. If we take the idea of self-transcendence *literally,* it is a contradiction in terms—it is logically incoherent. There is no way to form a clear, intelligible concept of it. The two words contain internally conflicting content—like a "round square." One can say the words, but what do they mean?

If we cannot see that for there to be transcendence, someone must be doing the transcending, we are obliged to confront the impossible question, Who is it that will experience the bliss promised to those who transcend their egos? The plain fact is, when self and ego go, *awareness* goes. And that condition is called unconsciousness or death.

We can talk about transcending a limited self-concept. We cannot talk—rationally—about transcending the self. We can talk about transcending an overrestricted concept of ego. We cannot talk—rationally—about transcending ego (not if we understand what ego really is and don't associate it with vanity or defensiveness).

What might confuse this issue for some people is a perfectly normal sense of self-forgetfulness or self-obliviousness that has nothing to do with the position I am discussing. For example, if we have good self-esteem we tend to be task-focused, not self-focused, a high percentage of the time, and certainly in the context of work. We do not typically sit at our desks thinking about how wonderful we are. But this does not mean we are selfless. It means the self is sufficiently secure for its value not to be an issue. Or again, if we sometimes choose to forego the ordinary pleasures of life because of a passion for our work, this is an act of self-expression, not self-surrender. If we sometimes choose to forego our own convenience or pleasure for the person we love, what deadlier insult could we deliver than to say we do so selflessly or self-sacrificially? The great compliment of love is that we identify our self-interest, in part, with the well-being of our partner. So we need to distinguish these behaviors from any notion of disappearing egos.

Interestingly enough, we encounter the denial of the reality of self or ego in a Western philosopher who would seem very distant from any mystical tradition—the British empiricist David Hume, who, in his *Treatise of Human Nature,* wrote:

> For my part, when I enter most intimately into what I call myself, *I always stumble on some particular perception or other,* of heat or cold, light or shade, love or hatred, pain or pleasure. I never catch myself *at any time without a perception, and never can observe anything but the perception.*[7]

From this, Hume concluded there is no such thing as a self or ego, since he was committed to the belief that only direct sensory evidence can confirm or disconfirm reality.

The Buddhist version is a little different, in that consciousness is not identified with a stream of sensory impressions. But both arguments share the idea that what exists is a stream of awareness and that the concept of a self or ego who is aware is superfluous and in fact fallacious. To quote W. T. Stace in *Mysticism and Philosophy:*

> This doctrine [of anatta or no-soul] rejects, by means of an argu-
> ment which is identical with the famous argument of David
> Hume, the whole concept of a self or soul. It argues that there is
> nothing in the mind but its empirical contents, and from this
> premise concludes, as Hume did, that the "I" is nothing but the
> stream of conscious states.[8]

Stace goes on to observe, a paragraph later, that "to wipe out the pure ego is to wipe out the mystical experience itself" because there is no one left to have the experience.

As long as there is consciousness, there is ego. As long as there is awareness, even at the highest level imaginable, there is self. After all our self-concepts have been transcended and all our attachments relinquished, as long as we exist as knowing, experiencing beings, in any sense whatsoever, the "I" who thinks, perceives, experiences—the "I" who is conscious—remains. (This in no way denies that as the individual evolves to higher and higher stages of development, the internal experience of "I" may be transformed.)

By way of responding to the Hume/Buddhist argument, I will point out that the demand that self or ego be an object of perception is itself an odd mistake. Since by *self* or *ego* in this ultimate sense we mean consciousness as it exists within an individual human being, it would be extraordinary—in fact, it would be *inconceivable*—for consciousness to be able to perceive itself. If consciousness is by nature an organ of perception, it is necessarily directed outward to something other than itself—just as our eyes are directed outward and cannot, without a mirror, see themselves. If our eyes could speak (in a world without mirrors) and said, in effect, "I see people and other objects but cannot see myself, so I have no grounds to assume I exist"—would that be a justifiable inference?

Furthermore, the very concept of consciousness depends on observations that there are entities—selves—who are conscious. In the development of a human mind, there would be no way to arrive at the idea of consciousness in the absence of such observations. Our entire understanding of the concept arose in the context of grasping that consciousness is an attribute of certain living organisms. We are not logically entitled to ignore that context and pretend to grab the idea of consciousness out of the air, as if it existed in a total vacuum—or as if there could be consciousness without anyone, human or animal, who was conscious. (It would be like using the concept of *elbow* while discarding as false or unnecessary the notion of anyone to whom the elbow belonged.) In Objectivist epistemology, this is called "the fallacy of the stolen concept"—with "consciousness," in this case, being the stolen concept.[9]

To elaborate: just as we cannot retain the concept of "orphan" while dropping the concept of "parent" on which it logically and genetically depends, so we are not entitled to use terms like "Consciousness," "Mind," or "Spirit"—as mystics do—while dropping the conceptual context that alone makes them meaningful, as in "consciousness without anyone who is conscious." Expressions like "Cosmic Consciousness" or "Universal Mind" or "Consciousness without an Object" (meaning consciousness without anything of which it is conscious) may sound like they mean something, but only until one asks oneself, "What, exactly?"

To quote Ayn Rand's admirably lucid formulation:

Existence exists [that which is, is]—and the act of grasping that statement implies two corollary axioms: that something exists which one perceives and that one exists possessing consciousness, consciousness being the faculty of perceiving that which exists.

If nothing exists, there can be no consciousness: a consciousness with nothing to be conscious of is a contradiction in terms. A consciousness conscious of nothing but itself is a contradiction in terms: before it could identify itself as consciousness, it had to be conscious of something. If that which you claim to perceive does not exist, what you possess is not consciousness.[10] (Emphasis added.)

Thus, whoever professes to be conscious is declaring, "I exist—and something other than me exists."

What cannot be asserted without logical absurdity is, "I am conscious—except that there is no 'I.' Self is an illusion."

One is reminded of the famous Cheshire cat from *Alice in Wonderland*—the smiling cat that disappears, leaving only the smile.

MYSTICISM: WHAT ARE ITS CLAIMS TO LEGITIMACY?

The mystical idea of self-transcendence is closely allied with the assertion that *separateness is a delusion.* According to this view, in reality "all is One." To experience this realization—so that all perceptions of separation, all "dualisms," all distinctions, *disappear* —is held to be the final triumph of consciousness. Stating the issue more personally, the goal of our spiritual evolution is to keep knocking down the ego-generated walls that produce the illusion of separateness from other things and beings in the universe until at last we arrive at a state of consciousness devoid of the experience of separateness, devoid of individuality, devoid of a sense of personal identity (except for identity with all that exists). Or better yet, the ideal is when all that is left is identity with "the Godhead," or the "Ultimate Ground of Being," or the "Suchness of Things." However formulated, the essential idea is that anything and everything pertaining to individuality *has got to go.*

As soon as we establish a boundary, the argument asserts, we create the possibility of an adversarial relationship. The self can go to war only with that which it regards as "the other," the non-self.

This may be true, but it is equally true to say that until we establish a boundary—that is, recognize individual identity—we cannot love. The self can love another self only if it can distinguish "the other" from itself. Even Narcissus had to imagine that his reflection was another person.

However, opponents of distinctions and boundaries insist, only when our sense of identity or of self expands to include everything that exists, only when we realize that we are all One, will all possibility of cruelty or hostility cease.

In *Mysticism and Philosophy*, W. T. Stace writes:

> *Hinduism, but more especially Buddhism, emphasizes that it is the separateness of each individual ego, and the clinging to this separateness, which is the root of hatred and of moral evil generally. . . . Only if the separate ego of each man is got rid of, if he can feel himself as not merely "I" but one with the life of all other individuals and with the life of God, only then can he hope for salvation.*

And also:

> *The basis of the mystical theory of ethics is that the separateness of individual selves produces egoism, which is the source of conflict, grasping, aggressiveness, selfishness, hatred, cruelty, malice, and other forms of evil; and that this separateness is abolished in the mystical consciousness in which all distinctions are annulled.*[11]

This idea is by no means confined to Buddhism or Hinduism. Many scholars assert that it can be found at the esoteric core of virtually all religious and mystical traditions.

Let me emphasize what the mystics are saying. They are *not* referring to that soul-stirring experience of being *connected* to everything that exists. This experience is sometimes described as feeling "at one with nature" or "at one with the universe." It is what some people mean when they speak of "feeling spiritual." Such feelings are *not* what the mystics mean when they talk of the abolition of separateness. To say "I feel at one with nature, or whatever," is still to recognize a distinction between self and nature or self and the universe. There is still me and what I feel at one with. What mystics are proposing is a state in which the distinction between self and not-self entirely disappears, and not just that distinction but also the distinction between apples and chairs, automobiles and clouds, adults and children, murdering and giving birth. *That* is the annulling of distinctions.

▲ ▲ ▲

**No human trait is more urgently needed for
survival than the ability to make distinctions.**

▼

Again, we must observe that when "separateness is abolished," not only hatred and cruelty but also kindness, compassion, generosity, admiration, and love will vanish—*because who will be there to inspire such feelings* and also *who will be there to feel them?* When identity goes, so does everything else.

No human trait is more urgently needed for survival than the ability to make distinctions. An infant's successful development requires grasping the fact of separateness. When separation and individuation significantly fail to occur, we have psychosis. Further, if we cannot distinguish between food and poison, we cannot exist. The more distinctions we are able to recognize, the more effectively we can navigate through the world. A mature individual is always aware of more distinctions than an immature one. A person who lives consciously is always aware of more distinctions than someone who does not. In *this* reality, in *this* world, the ability to perceive and respect distinctions is an absolute necessity. In what reality, in what world, is it *not* a necessity? How can it be a triumph of consciousness to achieve a state that, as long as one is in it, makes effective action impossible—a state that one has to come *out of* in order to function?

Even the ability to buy a book advocating the abolition of all distinctions requires the making of distinctions. Otherwise, one might buy a book upholding the importance of separateness.

Of course, no one has ever suggested that when fully "enlightened" beings—fully evolved or "realized" spiritual masters— move through the world, they do not need to make the same distinctions that the rest of us make. They recognize where their body ends and the door begins, just as you and I do. The difference, presumably, is that they simultaneously recognize that all such perceptions are illusory. This argument leads to a remarkable conclusion—namely, that if we are able to perceive reality correctly and if we act in accordance with that perception, we will no longer be able to function appropriately, no longer be able even to feed ourselves (since there will be no self to feed). What protects us at present is our blindness.

It has always seemed to most of us that we function better when our perceptions of reality are in alignment with the way reality actually is—and that when we act on the basis of illusion, delusion, or hallucination, we tend to suffer painful consequences. However, mystics inform us that at the highest stages of spiritual evolution, just the opposite is true. We are also informed that the inability to appreciate this wisdom is a limitation of our inadequately evolved minds.

The denial of the existence of real selves leads to severe intellectual difficulties. If the belief that I exist as a distinct entity is an illusion, surely it is *my* illusion, which means that in some form I exist. Even if it were claimed that I am only an illusion in someone else's consciousness, then that someone else would exist, and we would enter here into the problem of an infinite regress. And if it can be argued that all that ultimately exists is Cosmic Consciousness—which is what the mystics are saying, no matter how the position is formulated—then they are led to assert that Cosmic Consciousness (or God or Whatever) is confused about its own nature, is beset by illusions, is failing to grasp reality clearly. When one is ready to declare that the *Ultimate Ground of Being* or the *Suchness of Things* or *the Godhead* is deluded in its perception of reality, surely it is plain that one has collapsed into logical incoherence.

▲ ▼ ▲

However, mysticism is not necessarily troubled by logical incoherence. *Mysticism is the claim that there are aspects of existence that can be known by means of a unique cognitive faculty whose judgments are above the authority of sensory observation or reason.* In the domain over which the faculty asserts dominion—namely, the ultimate nature of reality—its authority is supreme and unbound by questions of evidence, proof, or logic.

A mystic might give an example such as this: When we look at a stick in water, the stick appears bent to us, but reason allows us to discover that in fact the stick is straight and that the illusion is caused by light rays traveling more slowly through water than through air; reason allows us to understand, not that our senses have deceived us, but that we have misinterpreted their evidence. However, we cannot grasp this if we limit ourselves to our senses —we need to shift to a higher level, the level of intellect. In much the same way, if we rely exclusively on reason and the evidence of the senses, we are limited in what we are able to comprehend; our grasp of reality will necessarily reflect error, at least some of the time—for example, all talk about God's nature inevitably breaks down in hopeless contradictions—and the only way out of that error is to shift to a still higher level of consciousness, the level of mystical insight, where all contradictions dissolve. I will examine this argument in a moment.

▲ ▼ ▲

One of the conclusions at which the great mystical traditions of the world tend to arrive is that the ultimate "stuff" of reality is not matter but consciousness or mind. "Mind is what there is and all there is," writes Ken Wilber in *Up from Eden,* "spaceless and therefore infinite, timeless and therefore eternal, outside of which nothing exists." [12] This metaphysical view has been embraced by many Western intellectuals, especially in the past few decades, in part as rebellion against the metaphysics of nineteenth-century materialism that has dominated so much of contemporary thought. The view is evidently seen as a step toward higher consciousness and greater spirituality.

Materialism is the doctrine that all that exists is matter and its motions. It maintains that all phenomena of consciousness can ultimately be "reduced" to these motions. Because the concept of "matter" has become increasingly troublesome and elusive in modern physics—one might say it has become "dematerialized"—many now prefer to say that all that exists is physical reality. Most of the books being written these days to "explain" mind or consciousness are written from this perspective or are heavily influenced by it.

However, we need to realize that these two theories do not exhaust the possibilities. We are not obliged to subscribe either to some form of Materialism or some form of Idealism. We are not compelled to seek to "reduce" consciousness to matter or matter to consciousness. We can justifiably maintain that neither matter nor consciousness is reducible to the other. There are powerful intellectual arguments against any such reductionism when there is no good reason to make the attempt. Metaphysically, mind and matter are *different.* But if they are different in every respect, the problem of explaining their interaction appears insuperable. How can mind influence matter and matter influence mind if they have absolutely nothing in common? And yet, that such reciprocal influence exists seems inescapable. This dilemma played a role in the attempt to reduce one of these two to the other.

Without going into details, I will suggest a possible way out. There is nothing inherently illogical—nothing that contradicts the rest of our knowledge—in positing some underlying reality of which both matter and consciousness are manifestations. The advantage of such a hypothesis is that it provides a means to resolve a problem that has troubled philosophers for centuries—"the mind-body problem," the problem of accounting for the interaction of consciousness and physical reality. If they have a common source, then they do have a point of commonality that makes their ability to interact less puzzling. How we would test this hypothesis, or provide justification for it, is another question. However, to call this underlying reality "God" or "Spirit" would clarify nothing and would further obscure what we are trying to understand.

▲▼▲

I want to pick up the thread of our basic purpose here. That purpose is to clarify the relationship between living consciously and spirituality. Since, today, any focus on spirituality leads us inevitably to the claims of mysticism, let us consider mysticism's basic assertion: that the natural evolution of consciousness is toward a spiritual breakthrough that liberates mind from the chains of logic and reason and achieves a superior, more reliable vision of reality.

Never mind that the contradictions it proclaims do total violence to consciousness itself. Never mind that such contradictions undercut the concept of reality at the deepest possible level. Never mind that the entire structure of human understanding rests on grasping the concept of identity as inherent in existence itself. (We saw all this in chapter 1). Never mind that many of the claims of mysticism are, in the literal sense, conceptually unintelligible and thus meaningless (in the same sense that the statement "In my new enlightenment I see that all squares are round" is unintelligible; internal contradictions collapse meaningfulness).

Let us set these objections aside for the moment. And let us ask: Why should we believe the mystics' claims? On what grounds? Why should we even continue the discussion?

To this inquiry, Wilber mounts an interesting answer. It is given in his book *Eye to Eye,* which is an attempt to justify the validity of knowledge attained through "the eye of contemplation," the mystic's alleged tool of cognition. I am choosing this argument as my focus because I regard it as the most ingenious I have encountered. I shall attempt to condense its essence to a few paragraphs.

The Christian mystic St. Bonaventure taught that there are at least three modes of attaining knowledge—"the *eye of the flesh,* by which we perceive the external world of space, time, and objects; the *eye of reason,* by which we attain a knowledge of philosophy, logic, and the mind itself; and the *eye of contemplation,* by which we rise to a knowledge of transcendent realities." [13]

Much error and chaos has afflicted human thought because of the "category error," which is the attempt of the eye of one domain to pronounce judgment on another. For example, this theory says, if we want to know the color of a wall, we *look*—we do not "reason" about it. If we want to grasp logical relationships, we *think*—we do not seek the answer with our senses. If we want to apprehend the nature of God, we shift to the eye of contemplation —we do not look to the senses or our intellect. When a mystic makes statements about the scientific world, such as how long the earth has existed, he is out of his proper domain and easily refuted by the scientist. When the scientist makes statements about transcendental realities, he is out of his proper domain, and his opinions are worthless.

However, Wilber argues, the principles by which knowledge is validated in the three domains are ultimately the same—this is his key point. Three steps are always involved in the verifying of knowledge. First, there is the *instrumental injunction*—"If you want to *know* this, do this." If you want to know if it's raining, go look. If you want to know how much is 36 times 36, go do the calculation. Then there is the *cognitive grasp*—the mind's apprehension of the data and its meaning. I see water falling; it is raining. I see that 36 times 36 equals 1296. Then there is the *communal confirmation*—checking the objectivity (the "intersubjectivity" would be Wilber's preferred term) of our knowledge by determining that others who traced our steps see the same things and arrive at the same conclusions.

All scientific conclusions reflect these three steps: we take actions of one kind or another that bring us into contact with certain data; we apprehend the meaning of the data; we ascertain that colleagues trained to reproduce our experiences—do the experiments, do the math, or whatever—arrive at the same final point. And thus is our knowledge confirmed. (And thus may it be *dis*confirmed—or at least put in question—if others who are qualified to reproduce our actions do so and find a different result.)

However—and here is a central point for the thesis—a person who is unable or unwilling to trace the scientist's steps is unqualified to pronounce judgment on the scientist's conclusions. Or, on a more primitive level, if I look out the window and say it's raining, and you refuse to look out the window while insisting it is *not* raining—your qualification to hold an opinion in this matter is not equal to mine. (Think of the men who, while claiming superior knowledge based on their religious beliefs, refused to look through Galileo's telescope.)

I will say only that this argument is correct—until and unless the scientist leaves the sphere of pure science and experimental data and begins offering metaphysical *interpretations* of the data that a nonscientist is entitled to challenge on logical grounds alone, as philosophers often do. And also, in the realm of science, it is possible for a lone genius to overturn many of the conclusions of the consensus of experts who have gone before. I am not aware that mysticism admits of such a possibility.

Insisting on the parallel between scientific and mystical knowledge, Wilber stresses that a competent mystic does not snatch his experience of reality out of the air. His experience reflects a long training and discipline that may entail years of meditation, prayer, and study, usually with a master teacher or a series of master teachers. Along the way, the student may imagine any number of "profound insights" that a teacher may gently dismiss, knowing them to be illusory or distractions from the main learning yet to be gained. Thus, mysticism is anything but an embrace of "whims" or "feelings." In fact, many mystics tend to be very severe about anything that looks like a mere whim or feeling. Eventually, when the training has advanced to a sufficient level, the student arrives at certain "illuminations" that are shared and confirmed by highly evolved or "realized" masters. The student (who is no longer a student) has now entered the domain of certified mystical knowledge.

And the process, we are told again and again, is in principle exactly the same as that by which one becomes a qualified scientist: knowledge is confirmed or disconfirmed according to whether qualified colleagues, having gone through the same steps, do or do not arrive at the same result. Experiments that are not reproducible or that do not yield the same results cannot be claimed to have revealed authentic truths. Therefore, in his or her own domain, the mystic's assertion of knowledge is fully as reliable as the scientist's.

And further: if we are not prepared to invest years of study, effort, and contemplative discipline, we are unable to trace the steps of the mystic's process—and if we cannot trace the steps of that process, we are unqualified to judge mysticism's claims. Also, if one embraces the mystic's claims merely out of, say, New Age enthusiasm—without the disciplined experience to back it up—that, too, is self-delusion; one is no more qualified to judge than a scientist/skeptic; one is in the playground of opinion or emotion, not knowledge. (In one of his books, Wilber writes that an atheist who struggles with the issue of God to the best of his rational understanding is "more spiritual" than one who embraces belief mindlessly, on blind faith.)

While this is only the bare essence of a fairly complex argument, it is sufficient to invite some basic and serious challenges. And since, please notice, every step of the argument is an appeal to *reason*—in that factual observations and logical inferences are offered in support of each point—the argument can be challenged on its own terms, in the court of observation and logic.

Note that the question is not whether mystics, after many years of meditation, prayer, study, or whatever, enter a state of consciousness in which they experience the world the way they describe. What would be the value of even arguing about that? The question is whether that state represents a valid claim to knowledge about reality.

There are a number of points that need to be made.

First, consider the situation of a five-year-old whose mental operations do not allow him access to certain understandings of reality that are available to say, his twelve-year-old brother. He simply has not developed to the stage where he can make sense, in terms of his own experience, of some of the things his brother tries to explain to him. However, in spite of this, why might he be inclined to grant credibility to some of his older brother's assertions? My answer is: because of something he *does* know in terms of his own experience (apart from the fact that his brother is bigger and older)—that his brother is better able to deal with and manipulate certain aspects of the world than he is; his brother functions at a higher level of competence, and the five-year-old recognizes this by his own firsthand judgment. So he may choose to take his older brother's advice even when he doesn't fully understand it.

Next, consider our relationship to sciences—say, physics and chemistry—about which our knowledge is rudimentary or nonexistent. We tend to grant high credibility to much of what physicists and chemists tell us, even though we have never traced the steps that led them to their conclusions. Why? Because we see by our own firsthand judgment that scientists know how to produce results we do not know how to produce and yet that we perceive to be valuable. They exhibit mastery over certain aspects of the world that we do not possess. And this may inspire some of us to follow in their tracks, to become a trained physicist or chemist, and learn one day to do what they can do and perhaps even go beyond it. We have a *reason* to study physics or chemistry that is meaningful and persuasive in terms of *our* observations, experience, and knowledge. We do not invest seven years of our life in earning a Ph.D. with absolutely no firsthand knowledge concerning the usefulness of the information we will acquire.

However, when we come to the knowledge claimed by mystics, the situation is entirely different. What are the areas of achievement or mastery of some aspect of the world that we can recognize in terms meaningful to us? What are they uniquely able to do that has significance for us, in terms of *our* understanding of the world, that might inspire us to think, "They know something I don't that really might be worth learning?" Apart from their teachings themselves, what is the area of unique perceivable competence that testifies to their superior wisdom? It is on this issue that the entire attempt to draw parallels with the stages of cognitive development or with the attainments of science breaks down.

If it be asserted that their achievements are *spiritual,* then we must point out that in order for the claim to be interesting to us, we must see some evidence that is meaningful *at our level of development,* as the achievements of science (via technology) are evident to a scientifically ignorant person.

If "realized" mystics, *as a class,* were uniquely able to accomplish things in this world that were incomprehensible within our context of knowledge yet were seen by us to be valuable, that would be grounds to want to learn how they did it. And some of us might pursue the path of meditation, prayer, or some other form of spiritual discipline relentlessly in order to find out. But in the absence of such grounds, what would our motivation be for such a long, difficult, and demanding effort?

That some individuals, for reasons they may or may not be able to articulate, might feel drawn to such a pursuit is not in question. In response to some inner feeling or need, any number of men and women have pursued one or another spiritual discipline. I do not judge that impulse or dismiss it as pathology, as many psychologists are prone to do. My point is this: if one is not already so inclined on one's own, what would constitute a good motivating reason?

Are mystics more serene than nonmystics? Sometimes, but not necessarily. There are serene atheists. Are mystics kinder, more generous, more compassionate? Sometimes, but not necessarily.

Cruelty is found among mystics, and compassion is found among many whose orientation is entirely secular. Are mystics superior to nonmystics in relieving human suffering? Hardly. In terms of improving the quality of life, conquering disease, creating jobs, building communities, providing protection against the hazards of nature, the great benefactors of humanity are scientists, inventors, and businesspersons, whose productive concerns are this-worldly. Does a life devoted to spiritual discipline in the mystical sense produce a superior moral character? Not necessarily. There have been renowned spiritual teachers, judged by their peers to be fully "realized," fully enlightened, who were drunkards, embezzlers, exploiters of their followers, seducers of very young male and female acolytes.

When I raised this last issue once with a gentleman from India, he remarked that just as there is no intrinsic connection between high intellectual development and moral character—a genius can be a psychopath—so there is no intrinsic connection between being at a high level of spiritual development, in the mystical sense, and being an ethical individual. He added that spiritual work could perhaps *incline* one to a superior moral path but could not guarantee it, no matter how enlightened one might be. I agreed, and said, "Doesn't that disturb you? Don't you find that a bit strange?" He sighed, "Well, what can I tell you, Nathaniel?"

I related a story about a world-famous Indian guru, Swami Muktananda, whom I first met in the mid-1970s, when he had an ashram in the Catskills. At that time, he was held by many educated people to be one of the most spiritually enlightened beings on the planet. His credentials, by standards set forth above, were impeccable. I had heard about him and was curious. At that point, I had read almost nothing in the field of mysticism and had decided to begin correcting my ignorance. I wanted to observe and experience a renowned guru "in the flesh." I was greeted warmly by the publicity director and given a privileged seat up front in a huge meditation hall. I rather liked the quality of Muktananda's being—especially his aura of absolute self-acceptance (or so it seemed that day)—and found many of the things he had to say quite interesting. Some of his psychological observations in particular I thought valid and useful. (I do not contend that mystics have never contributed useful insights.) While in no sense a convert, I was curious, as a psychologist, to observe more, and I decided to come back with my wife, Patrecia, to participate in one of Muktananda's weekend "intensives." While visiting New York without me, Patrecia had been taken to the ashram before by a friend who had merely told her, "Let's go for a weekend in the country." She was already known to Muktananda, and he was rather friendly and playful with her. Patrecia was then working as a model while pursuing a career in acting, and a great many magazines carried her picture in one particular ad (for Salem cigarettes, if I recall correctly). During the weekend she and I were there together, someone showed Muktananda the ad featuring Patrecia's face. He became very enthusiastic, and word went out over loudspeakers that he wanted to see her. Later, somewhat deflated, she said to me, "He became excited over the ad, as if I were a movie star or something. He suddenly seemed so shallow, like some small-town innocent who thinks modeling is 'glamorous.' I couldn't believe the way he was acting. And there was something else that really turned me off: I felt sexual vibrations coming at me. I didn't like the way he hugged me." This surprised me, as Muktananda made a strong point of his commitment to celibacy. "Are you sure you didn't imagine it?" I asked. "I'm sure," she answered. That was the end of her interest in him. Years later, when Patrecia had died and I had remarried, Muktananda came to Southern California and set up a facility in Santa Monica. It was then that I first began hearing the rumors, which grew stronger over the next several years. Eventually, the story came out —of his sexual seduction of thirteen-year-old female worshippers, under the guise, I believe, of making some sort of spiritual connection with them or giving them a spiritual "gift" through his body. A number of his followers subsequently left his service in disillusionment and disgust, some with their own stories to tell of a

Muktananda very different from his public persona. "There's no denying it," said the gentleman from India. "Those things do happen."

What I wish to stress is that we were not talking about some local priest who molests children. We were talking about a spiritual leader who was held to be *supremely realized,* who had made it all the way to the top of the spiritual/mystical mountain, who allegedly operated at the highest level of consciousness. That there are mystics who in their dealings with others exhibit high moral character is not in contention here. But what we must understand is that the vision of "highly evolved consciousness" projected by mystics does not *necessarily* demand a high level of personal integrity as one of the proofs of enlightenment.

As an aside, I will mention that such a viewpoint is entirely incompatible with the concept of living consciously developed in this book: I would not say of a person who conspicuously lacked integrity that he nonetheless had mastered the art of living consciously.

In chapter 1, I said that the battle cry of reason is "Integrate!" What I found especially fascinating in the justification offered above for the knowledge claims of mysticism is that at every step the appeal is to reason and observation. The entire thesis is a long exercise in attempted logical integration, full of "becauses" and "therefores." And in the end, what is the justification offered for accepting the mystics' insights? In essence, the argument is this: Since all knowledge is built on taking specific actions, making observations, grasping the meaning or implications of those observations, checking one's conclusions with the community of competently trained colleagues—and since this is the basic pattern of science and equally the basic pattern of mysticism—then mystical insights that follow the required actions, observations, and cognitive grasping and are shared and confirmed by the community of one's peers are legitimately proclaimed *knowledge.* In other words, it is *reasonable* to accept the truth of such insights. *Reason is still conceded to be the final arbiter.* "It is logical to accept these nonlogical, nonrational insights because . . . "

That I regard the argument as fallacious is not my point here. My point is that, if one argues at all, there is no escape from using and counting on the very faculty mystics profess to have evolved "beyond." And this is the ultimate dilemma of anyone who is too conscientious simply to proclaim "It's true because I feel it."

We may not always arrive at our insights by a process of reason, but reason is the means by which we ultimately verify them—by what is sometimes called "reality testing"—that is, integrating them into the rest of our knowledge and observations without contradiction. An appreciation of this truth is an essential element of what I mean by living consciously.

So what are we left with? A collection of assertions about the ultimate nature of existence that are riddled with contradictions, defy reason and logic, convey no intelligible meaning, invalidate our consciousness, destroy our concept of reality—and that we are meant to take seriously while being told our limited development makes it impossible for us to understand them. If one does not have an intellectual inferiority complex and is not easily intimidated, this is not impressive.

▲ ▼ ▲

Many more objections can be made to the mystics' case. My analysis is far from exhaustive. But this is not a treatise on mysticism, and I believe the observations I have made are sufficient for our purposes.

So let us consider, finally, the identification of "spirituality" with the ethics of selflessness—a doctrine offered to us as an expression of the superior wisdom to be found "beyond reason."

SELFLESSNESS: RETHINKING
OUR BASIC ASSUMPTIONS AND
DISCOVERING ENLIGHTENED SELFISHNESS

In an ethical context, "selflessness" means devoid of, or untainted by, self-interest. So to behave selflessly is to act without concern for any benefit to oneself. This is commonly regarded as the essence of morality. It is presumed to be the way that "spiritually evolved" people behave. Indeed, such behavior is sometimes taken as *evidence* of one's "spirituality."

Let us see if this doctrine is compatible with the principle of living consciously.

Observe, first of all, that in equating unselfishness with morality, the implication is that self-interested actions are either immoral or nonmoral. That is, they are either bad or without moral significance. If, for instance, I protest paying taxes to support programs of which I do not approve, then according to this code I am being selfish and therefore immoral. If I work to support myself, that is not immoral but neither is it admirable; it is ethically neutral.

This doctrine takes for granted—as self-evident—a clash between self-interest and morality: we can pursue our self-interest or we can be moral, but we can't be both. And it upholds self-sacrifice as the ideal. Sometimes this ideal is expressed as "a life of selfless service."

As one psychologist puts it:

> As [spiritual] awakening begins, motivations inevitably shift from the egocentric toward the desire to serve others. This kind of service is seen as absolutely necessary if the awakening and development are to continue; [spiritual] growth requires a life of service.[14]

What is significant about this viewpoint concerning the evil of "selfishness" is in how many versions it has appeared throughout human history. Don't be selfish—subordinate your interests to those of the tribe. Don't be selfish—subordinate your interests to those of the family. Don't be selfish—sacrifice for the Pharaoh, Emperor, King, Church, Country, Race, State, Proletariat, Society, or Globe. Remember: *Service* is your noblest goal; *selfishness* is the root of all evil.

In this doctrine, selfishness is presumed to be narrow, petty, small-minded, materialistic, immature, narcissistic, anti-social, exploitative, mean-spirited, arrogant, ruthless, indifferent, cruel, and potentially murderous. These traits are evidently regarded as being to one's self-interest, since they are labeled as expressions of selfishness. It is interesting to speculate about the psychology of those who believe this. By my own very different concept of morality I would say these traits are self-destructive—and that self-destruction is not to one's self-interest.

▲▲▲

What is this book but an attempt to demonstrate that living consciously—clearly a moral as well as a psychological ideal—is to one's selfish interest?

▼

If one's goal is a happy and fulfilling life, self-interest is best served by rationality, productivity, integrity, and a sense of justice and benevolence in dealings with others. It is served by learning to think long-range and to project the consequences of one's actions, which means learning to live self-responsibly. Irresponsibility is *not* to one's self-interest. And neither is mindlessness, dishonesty, or brutality.

What is this book but an attempt to demonstrate that living consciously—clearly a moral as well as psychological ideal—is to one's selfish interest?

In taking for granted a conflict between morality and self-interest, exponents of self-sacrifice and selfless service assume, first of all, that no one could have a selfish interest in being moral, and second, that the purpose of morality is not to serve the individual's well-being but to subordinate it to allegedly higher ends. These are the necessary presuppositions of the idea that morality equals selflessness. This doctrine says to the individual: Your life does not belong to you; you are not an end in yourself but only a means to the ends of others; you are here to serve; you have no right to exist for your own sake. What is remarkable is that when this moral vision is offered in a religious context, it is identified as an expression of "love for man."

▲▼▲

Consider the following example. A young woman—I will call her Marny—decides she would like to become an architect. Her father is deeply disappointed, because he had always dreamed that after college she would join him in the dress business. "Must you be so selfish?" Marny's mother says to her. "You're breaking your father's heart."

"If I don't study architecture," Marny answers, "I'll break my own heart."

So Marny goes to college to become an architect. While at college, she dates a young man who falls in love with her. He begs her to marry him, give up architecture, and become the mother of his children. "In the first place," Marny tells him gently, not wishing to cause pain, "I don't love you. And in the second place, I don't plan to have children, at least not in the foreseeable future."

"Not have children?" the young man cries. "How can you be so selfish? And don't you care at all about my happiness?"

"Don't you care at all about mine?" she responds, smiling.

A few years later, now a practicing architect, she meets a man with whom she falls in love. Marny sees in him the embodiment of the traits she most admires: strength, self-confidence, integrity, and a passionate nature unafraid of love or intimacy. To marry him, share her excitement and joy with him, nurture him at times, support him in his struggles as he supports her in hers—join with him in fighting for causes in which they both believe—is experienced by her as selfish in the most natural and benevolent sense of the word. She is living for *her* values. Her life is productive, stimulating, and filled with love.

So when her husband becomes ill, for a long time she curtails many of her activities to take care of him. When friends praise her for her "unselfishness," she looks at them incredulously. "I *love* him" is her only answer. The thought of selfless service would not occur to her. She would not insult what she feels for her husband by calling her caretaking self-sacrifice. "Not if you hold the full context," she explains. "What would I do if I were 'selfish?' Abandon him? Whose notion of self-interest is that?"

Later, when her husband recovers and life has stabilized again, she returns to work with great passion. She is eager to make up for lost time. When certain of her friends call to discuss personal problems, she accommodates them for a while, but when she realizes how much of her energy is being drained by them she finally calls a halt. "Sorry," she says. "I don't want to disappoint you, but right now I've got more urgent priorities."

"God, but you're selfish," she is told.

When she deals with other human beings, she respects the legitimacy of their self-interest and does not expect them to sacrifice it, any more than she would sacrifice her own. And she cannot understand why other people do not necessarily feel this way.

She notices that "selfish" is what some people call her when she is doing what she wants to do rather than what they want her to do. She also notices that while she is not intimidated by this accusation, many others are.

Question: Is Marny a virtuous woman or an unvirtuous one? Is she moral or immoral? Clearly, she is not an altruist. But then what is she? What can we say about her?

The first thing I would say about her is that she operates *consciously.* And the next thing I would say is that she stands outside traditional moral categories: she is an exponent of rational or enlightened self-interest—a possibility not even acknowledged by those who talk about self-sacrifice as the moral ideal and imply that the only alternative to sacrificing self to others is sacrificing others to self. Marny does neither; she does not believe in the practice of human sacrifice.

Observe that everything she does is motivated by loyalty to *her* values. She acts on *her* judgment. And her judgment is thoughtful, not impulsive. For her husband, whom she loves most in the world, there are almost no limits on what she is prepared to do (within a rational framework). For her friends, there are many more limits; she is generous, but not to the point of ignoring her higher values. If she supports certain causes, it is because they concern values that are important to *her* and to the kind of world she wishes to live in. She respects self-interest but understands that what is or is not to one's self-interest is not necessarily self-evident —it requires thought. And her range of concern is a lifetime, not the convenience or inconvenience of this moment. That is why I say she operates consciously.

The philosopher Immanuel Kant would tell her she is immoral, since everything she does is by selfish inclination. Kant taught that any action contaminated by self-interest to even the smallest degree can make no claim to moral merit—only that which is done out of *duty* can be virtuous. Hitler would tell her she has no right to live for herself, that her life is owed to the German race, and that the pursuit of personal happiness leads only to suffering. Stalin would tell her that her petty bourgeois preoccupations are absurd, that her egoistic inclinations are subversive, and that her life belongs not to herself but to the Proletariat, meaning the State. Mao would tell her it is evil and irresponsible for her to imagine that her person is her property—she must accept that she is to be disposed of as the People see fit. The Pope would tell her that her practice of birth control is sinfully egocentric. A New Age psychologist enamored with the wisdom of the East might tell her she is retarded in her spiritual development because she still thinks of her happiness in terms of the narrowly personal. And a mystic would tell her that if she dedicates unknown years of her life to meditation, prayer, and study, eventually the veil of ignorance will fall away and she will grasp that selfishness is indeed the root of all evil and that only through selfless service can her soul fully awaken.

▲ ▼ ▲

Now, if we want to talk about evil, I will say that these teachings are what I regard as evil—because of the consequences to which they lead for human life on earth.

No one inveighed against "selfishness" or advocated "selfless service" more passionately than the leaders of Nazi Germany, the Soviet Union, Communist China, or Cambodia. Take a look at what those "ideals" mean when translated into political reality. More people have been tortured and murdered in this century than any other in history, and the justification was always "in the name of a higher good to which the individual must be subordinated." Hitler, Stalin, Mao, and Pol Pot taught their people a lot about "selfless service."

It could be argued that whatever may be true about the cases just cited, it does not apply to Buddhists, who are probably the most peaceful, nonviolent people on the planet. This is correct, and it is a fair point to raise. However, consider this: if we teach that individuality is an illusion and that service to others is the essence of morality, what kind of cultural and intellectual climate do we help create? One that serves a society built on the principles of individual freedom and individual rights—or a society that proclaims duty to the collective above all? Is the doctrine of selfless service more likely to protect an individual when freedom is threatened, or make the individual more vulnerable to manipulation and control?

▲ ▲ ▲

How many people give up their dreams and aspirations in deference to the needs and demands of others because they dread the charge of being egocentric?

▼

Anyone who practices psychotherapy almost certainly knows how frightened many people are of even the most appropriate acts of self-assertiveness—they do not know how to answer the charge that they are being selfish. How many people die in insane wars because they do not want to admit they care more about their own lives than about some abstract cause that may make no sense to them? How many people give up their dreams and aspirations in deference to the needs and demands of others because they dread the charge of being egocentric? This is an open secret: almost everyone knows it and almost no one talks about it. Instead, we go on insisting that ego is the cause of all our misery.

In the course of everyday life, we are bombarded in a thousand ways with messages to the effect that "service" is the highest mark of virtue and that morality consists of living for others. We are told that the intelligent, the enlightened, the able, the competent, the strong must exist for the sake of those who lack those traits; that those who suffer or are in need have first claim on the lives and energy of the rest of the human race, that theirs is the right superseding all other rights. We are told that an individual's mind and effort are the property of the community, the nation, the globe. We are told that those who have created wealth owe a particular debt to those who have not created it—including an apology. And all the while politicians, religious leaders, and intellectuals subtly or not so subtly chastise the electorate for being too reluctant to sacrifice for the greater good.

Most people do not try to practice the code of self-sacrifice consistently in their everyday choices and decisions. That would not be possible. But to the extent that they accept it as *right,* they are left in confusion, if not in a moral vacuum. They have no adequate set of principles to guide their actions. In relationships, they do not know what demands they can permit themselves and what demands they can permit to others; they do not know what is theirs by right, theirs by favor, or theirs by someone's sacrifice. Under the pressure of conflicting personal desires and conflicting external injunctions, they fluctuate between sacrificing themselves to others and sacrificing others to themselves. They swing between the belief that self-surrender is a virtue and the knowledge that they must smuggle *some* selfishness into their lives in order to survive.

Small wonder that when some people do decide to be selfish, they are so often selfish in the narrow and petty sense rather than in the rational and noble sense. No one taught them that *rational* self-interest is possible—and that it is the obligation of a conscious human being to think carefully about what does in fact represent long-term self-interest. When they hear selfishness castigated as petty, cruel, materialistic, anti-social, or mean-spirited, these epithets strike a responsive chord within them: their own guilt feels like a validation of the charge.

This discussion is a brief exercise in what I meant earlier in this book when I suggested that if our intention is to live consciously, we need to focus the searchlight of awareness on the moral values we have been taught since childhood—to look at moral issues through our own eyes—and consider what serves our life and well-being and what is inimical. However, this is not the place for a full moral treatise. I have explored different aspects of value theory in previous books, notably *Honoring the Self* and *The Six Pillars of Self-Esteem,* and plan to address these issues in greater depth in a future book. Here, I need to make only a few more points about the identification of spirituality with an ethics of selflessness.

▲ ▼ ▲

If we are operating consciously, the most obvious question to ask, when someone proposes "a life of selfless service," is *why?*

To quote Ayn Rand in *Atlas Shrugged:*

> *Why is it moral to serve the happiness of others, but not your own? If enjoyment is a value, why is it moral when experienced by others, but immoral when experienced by you? ... Why is it immoral for you to desire, but moral for others to do so? Why is it immoral to produce a value and keep it, but moral to give it away? And if it is not moral for you to keep a value, why is it moral for others to accept it? If you are selfless and virtuous when you give it, are they not selfish and vicious when they take it? Does virtue consist of serving vice?* [15]

Those who tend to associate spirituality with selfless service typically offer two answers to the question of *why?* The first is not really an answer. It consists of the assertion that at a certain level of spiritual evolution, one gains the mystical insight—as a self-evident fact, requiring no further explanation—that one should take the path of selfless service. It becomes as obvious as the sun hanging in the sky—one simply *sees* it. This is not an explanation likely to impress a thoughtful person.

The second, and by far the more interesting explanation, is the statement that the value of such service lies not so much in the help given the beneficiaries as in *liberation from ego* on the part of the one who serves. A life of service, it is said, facilitates self-transcendence. In secular terms, this is dangerously close to an egoistic justification: I will serve others as a means to personal development.

I confess I am not really clear on what a life of selfless service literally means. I cannot find a plain definition anywhere. Do we ask people what they would like us to do and then do it (like a solicitous "pleaser")? Do we decide what we think is best for them and do that (like a totalitarian altruist)? Does it mean we abandon the life and work we chose before we attained liberation from ego and go searching the world for suffering to ameliorate (like anyone for whom self-surrender is glory)?

What also confuses me is that I have known a number of prominent intellectuals who became professors, wrote books, and then, at some point, saw the light and embraced the ideal of selfless service. They are still professors and they still write books, and in their books they talk about the ideal of service—but apart from that I cannot see how their life has changed. Whom are they serving, and how are they doing it? (Some of them have become social activists dedicated to saving the world from capitalism, about which they know appallingly little.)

Perhaps I will be asked: But is not the justification for a life of service the fact that there is so much suffering in the world? Are not kindness and compassion virtues even in your morality?

▲ ▲ ▲

Why would anyone identify kindness or
compassion with self-sacrifice? If it is in the

> name of one's values—such as regard for the
> value of human life—kindness can be as much
> an act of self-assertion as any other act of
> self-expression.
>
> ▼

The answer to the second question is yes, kindness and compassion are virtues. We cannot have a decent life without them. But why would anyone identify kindness or compassion with self-sacrifice? If it is in the name of one's values—such as regard for the value of a human life—kindness can be as much an act of self-assertion as any other act of self-expression. And yes, there is a great deal of suffering in the world. And one of the reasons for that suffering is the fact that most people have never been taught a code of ethical principles that would support a truly *human* form of existence on earth. Consider the following.

▲ ▼ ▲

One of the greatest causes of suffering on this planet is poverty. It follows, therefore, that if one is genuinely interested in relieving suffering and is disposed to approach the problem consciously, one would wish to understand how poverty can be eliminated. Fortunately, the answer is known.

Prior to the industrial revolution and the birth of capitalism, poverty was the natural condition of almost all of the human race. It was not perceived as an aberration but as the norm. Ninety-eight percent of the world's population lived in conditions unimaginable to a twentieth-century citizen of the United States. *That* was poverty of a kind that makes what we call poverty today look like luxury. Then, dating from the time of the American Revolution, the ideas of individualism, human rights, and political/economic freedom—*capitalism*—began to sweep the Western world. To the extent that capitalism was accepted, which varied enormously from country to country, the result was an unprecedented rise in the standard of living of millions and millions of people that would have been inconceivable a century earlier. Infant mortality rates dropped, and life expectancy leapt upward. In the brief span of less than two hundred years the West witnessed a growth in material well-being unequaled by the sum of human progress up to that time. At every step of the way, the freer the country was, the faster the rate of progress and the more rapid the decline of poverty.

What compassionate mystic understood what he was seeing, above all in the United States, stopped talking about self-sacrifice, decided to step out of the Middle Ages and rethink his code of values—and began proclaiming the glories that were possible when human intelligence is liberated and people are free to act on their own initiative? What compassionate mystic—hit by a *this*-worldly vision—got enlightenment and realized that there might be an answer to suffering this side of Nirvana and began to champion the right of life, liberty, property, and the pursuit of happiness?

Notice, even today, with the worldwide collapse of collectivist economies, how grudgingly the Vatican acknowledges the achievements of free minds and semi-free markets in raising the quality of our lives. Notice the resentment that still attaches to the word *profit* by glowering, cassocked Rip van Winkles who still think they are living in the year 1200 and have not yet discovered the industrial age, let alone the information age. Notice the arrogant presumptuousness of offering miserly recognition to entrepreneurs who have transformed the world—and immediately following it by scolding reminders that they are, after all, only servants of humanity and should not be allowed to forget it.

To carry this point still further: a major part of the world that for a very long time fiercely resisted the incursion of "Western ideas" is Asia, and this is an area where the influence of mysticism has been at its strongest and where for centuries poverty has been at its worst. But in the years following World War II, the situation began to change. Slowly, the ideas of entrepreneurial capitalism caught fire in the Asian mind. Men (and women!) of courage, initiative, and ambition began to challenge old traditions and think about the possibilities of this world, if governments would cede them even a modest degree of economic and political freedom. They got a little freedom, and then they pressed for a little more and a little more. The battle is still going on and is far from over. But what has happened has been described as a miracle.

To quote from John Naisbitt's *Megatrends Asia:*

> From 1945 to 1995, half a century, Asia went from rags to riches. It reduced the incidence of poverty from 400 million to 180 million, while its population grew by 400 million during the same period. The World Bank has pronounced that nowhere and at no time in human history has humanity achieved such economic progress, and concluded that the East Asia story is an economic miracle.[16]

A significant aspect of this story is the cultural transformation in the role of women. An increasing number of Asian women have become entrepreneurs, against thousands of years of tradition. And more and more women are pouring into the workplace. (In Japan, for example, virtually all the currency traders are women.) To be sure, there is still much resistance to these changes, and there are still efforts to integrate Asia's semicapitalism into "the old ways," resulting in some rather incongruous mixtures of practices and principles. That is culturally inevitable. In addition, there is still a good deal of dangerous financial and political instability in these countries that makes their future progress far from automatic. But an extravagant source of human energy has been released by such freedom as has been permitted and is not likely to be bottled up again.

In an age in which few achievements seem to impress us and the most extraordinary triumphs of human intelligence often leave us blasé, take a moment to meditate on the meaning of the quote from Naisbitt. And then ask yourself:

Why aren't the apostles of kindness, compassion, and concern for human suffering shouting about this historic achievement from the rooftops?

Why are they not celebrating the nobility of the entrepreneurial spirit and the power of the liberated mind to accomplish "miracles"?

Why are they not championing such life-serving virtues as independence, productive ambition, competence, self-responsibility, self-assertiveness, integrity, and the drive to innovate?

▲▲▲

It is not kindness, compassion, or selflessness that lift people out of poverty. It is liberated human ability—combined with perseverance, courage, and the desire to achieve something worthwhile and (sometimes) make money in the process.

▼

Instead, they still talk as if we lived in preindustrial times, before anyone grasped that wealth could be *created,* when all one could do at best was share one's meager subsistence with a fellow sufferer, and the first traders and businessmen were looked on with scorn because of their concern with "material" reality. Perhaps, then, in the darkness and despair of the times, kindness and compassion were just about all human beings could offer one another. Certainly they could not project new industries that would offer employment to millions of people, build communities, heal poverty, and create undreamed-of possibilities of survival and well-being. But today the evidence is all around us—and if it is not acknowledged and appreciated, then we have to wonder whether the amelioration of suffering is really the primary agenda of these exponents of enlightenment or whether other agendas are operating within them that enjoy a higher priority. With the best will in the world, I am unable to believe that blindness of this magnitude can be innocent.

It is not kindness, compassion, or selflessness that lift people out of poverty. It is liberated human ability—combined with perseverance, courage, and the desire to achieve something worthwhile and (sometimes) make money in the process. But of course, such motives are not unselfish. And that is why they can accomplish "miracles."

Kindness and compassion are virtues, to be sure, but what has carried the world and moved it forward, lifting humankind out of the cave and beyond a life expectancy of twenty-four—what has conquered disease and steadily lightened the burden of human existence—what has created and goes on creating new possibilities for fulfillment and joy on earth—is the rational, self-assertive egos of audaciously imaginative men and women who refuse to accept suffering and stagnation as our destiny.

If you doubt it, drop all our selfless politicians, social activists, and mystics into some jungle where people still live as they lived hundreds of thousands of years ago, barely able to scratch out subsistence and at the helpless mercy of every upheaval of nature, and invite these visiting humanitarians to create abundance.

"Even if everything you say is true," I am sometimes asked, "hasn't our progress generated *new* problems, new dislocations, instabilities, and dangers?" The answer is that *every* step of human progress creates new difficulties and challenges, and they can and will be overcome, but not by cursing the virtues that made the progress possible, not by curtailing the freedom that allows intelligence to function.

"But isn't there more to life than mere material reality?" The short answer is, of course. For a slightly longer answer, I will quote a favorite passage of mine from *Atlas Shrugged:*

> *You, who claim that you long to rise above the crude concerns of the body, above the drudgery of serving mere physical needs— who is enslaved by physical needs: the Hindu who labors from sunrise to sunset at the shafts of a hand-plow for a bowl of rice, or the American who is driving a tractor? Who is the conqueror of physical reality: the man who sleeps on a bed of nails or the man who sleeps on an inner-spring mattress? Which is the monument to the triumph of the human spirit over matter: the*

*germ-eaten hovels on the shorelines of the Ganges or the Atlantic
skyline of New York?* [17]

I will add: and if India has become economically more developed than it was forty-plus years ago, when the above passage was first published—if, for example, once-starving India has now become an *exporter* of food—*who* are the persons responsible: those who preached the renunciation of ego or those who fought for greater freedom for the individual? Those who lead ashrams or those who lead research institutes and business enterprises? Those who stare at another dimension or those who work to transform this one?

If ego is the unifying center of consciousness, the faculty within us that thinks, judges, wills, and drives the process of achievement, then—before embracing selflessness as an ideal—reflect on the nature of a world from which ego has vanished and consider whether it is a world in which you would wish to exist.

Right here, right now, is an opportunity to live consciously.

Afterword

LOOKING back over a career that has spanned four decades, I see how consistently the underlying theme of my work, implicit in everything I have written, has been one central message: *Your life is important. Whether you achieve what you want in life matters. Whether you are happy matters. Honor and fight for your highest potential. Self-realization—the realization of the best within you—is the noblest goal of your existence.* The rest of my writing has been devoted to the philosophical and psychological elaboration of this perspective as well as to identifying the practical steps by which it can be implemented. This project led inevitably to a focus on the role of the mind in human well-being.

Mind is a survival tool in more ways than most of us understand. A few weeks ago I read a report on aging to the effect that older members of the population who keep themselves intellectually challenged or find some active use for their minds optimize their chances of living longer. Other things being equal, a person who stays mentally active tends to enjoy a longer life span than a person who is mentally passive. Further, there is evidence that continuous intellectual stimulation and new learning may tend to make one less susceptible to the ravages of Alzheimer's disease.

Unfortunately, ours is in many respects an anti-intellectual culture, one that impedes the development of mind far more than supports it. On the academic level, an example of what I mean is the assaults on reason, logic, and objectivity in our philosophy departments, which have all but resulted in the demise of philosophy as a serious discipline (a problem I shall address in a future book). On the popular level, an example is the content of most of our television programs. It has been found that watching large quantities of television is not conducive to the intellectual development of young people; often it retards such development (and thereby militates against living consciously). With regard to this latter problem, one solution is for parents to limit the amount of television children are allowed to watch. Another, indicated in an earlier chapter, may take more effort on the part of parents but is no less important: teaching young people *how* to look at television (or movies), how to grasp implications, how to recognize hidden messages, non sequiturs, contradictions, and multiple forms of misleading propaganda. (Examples: taking mind-altering drugs is smart, sophisticated, "cool"; physical violence is the most practical way to solve most problems; government officials are chiefly motivated by noble intentions while businesspeople are chiefly motivated by evil ones.) Of course, to teach their children, parents have to be able to recognize such messages themselves. Unconsciousness, no less than consciousness, can be passed or at least encouraged from one generation to another.

If our goal is to learn to live at a high level of awareness, nothing may be more important than discarding the notion that consciousness is a burden and grasping instead that it is a source of liberation, empowerment, and increased possibilities. The more conscious we are, the more options we are aware of in any situation. The less conscious we are, the fewer the options of which we are likely to be aware. Another way of saying this is to observe that the more conscious we are, the more resourceful in meeting life's challenges.

And confidence in our ability to meet life's challenges is a basic human need. Such confidence is one of the core meanings of self-esteem—trust in our ability to think, learn, make decisions, cope with the unfamiliar, and master difficulties—which requires a mind committed to awareness. When we avoid awareness in contexts where awareness is needed, there is no mystery why we so often experience insecurity and anxiety. We face life disarmed and know we have done it to ourselves.

To live consciously is not always easy. But—looked at in the full context of a life span—the alternative is much harder.

▲ ▲ ▲

If our goal is to learn to live at a high level of awareness, nothing may be more important than discarding the notion that consciousness is a burden and grasping instead that it is a source of liberation, empowerment, and increased possibilities.

▼

The problem is, when we do not live consciously, we often fail to appreciate how much of our suffering is attributable to that fact. We do not see the connection between our avoidance of awareness and the emptiness of our marriage, the unhappiness of our children, the disappointments in our career, our anxieties in the face of change, our chronic boredom and fatigue, the unresolved conflicts that tear us apart, or our impoverished self-esteem. Our thinking never gets deeper than "There's something wrong with me" or "There's something wrong with the world" or "Why doesn't life make more sense?" or "Why me, God?" And too often, our response to frustration and pain is to shrink our consciousness still further—to make life bearable, we imagine—as we sink deeper and deeper into the void of the unreached and unfulfilled. One of the reasons some of us fear death as much as we do is our secret knowledge of how incompletely we have lived.

▲ ▲ ▲

**Living consciously is an act of love for one's
own positive possibilities. It is an act of
commitment to one's value as a person and to
the importance of one's life.**

▼

Living consciously is not a duty we owe others, although others
will often benefit from our greater awareness and sensitivity. It is
a responsibility we owe to ourselves. It is an act of love for one's
own positive possibilities. It is an act of commitment to one's value
as a person and to the importance of one's life.

For these reasons, you might find it useful to ask yourself: With
what level of consciousness and mental focus did I read this book?
How open was I to arguments and perspectives that perhaps were
unfamiliar to me? If certain passages made me uncomfortable, did
that inspire me to go unconscious or to read them more thoughtfully? Do I treat discomfort as a signal to shut my eyes or to open
them wider?

If passages made you anxious or angry or bored or irritable,
those are the ones it is probably most relevant to read again.

I will go further and suggest, most respectfully, that if you now
feel you clearly understand the practice of living consciously, that
is the ideal state of mind in which to begin reading this book again
from the beginning. This book contains doors that sometimes open
only at the second or third touch of the handle.

APPENDIX

A Sentence-Completion Program to Facilitate Living Consciously

Throughout this book, I have given examples of the use of the sentence-completion technique to expand awareness. Below are sets of exercises that can assist you in the project of deepening your awareness in various areas of your life.

The essence of the sentence-completion procedure, as we will use it here, is to write an incomplete sentence, a sentence stem, and to keep adding endings—*not less than six, and ten is sufficient*—as fast as possible, with the sole requirement that each ending be a grammatical completion of the sentence.

Work as rapidly as possible—speed is essential—no pauses to "think," no censoring, *inventing if you get stuck,* without worrying if any particular ending is literally true, reasonable, or significant. *Any* ending is fine. *Just keep going.*

The art of doing sentence completion well is to maintain a high level of mental focus combined with a total lack of inner inhibition. Doing this work on a daily basis as described here is a kind of psychological discipline that over time allows us to achieve insight, integration, and often spontaneous behavior change.

People sometimes ask, "How do I integrate the things I am becoming conscious of?" The answer is that the practice itself, done repetitively, tends to bring about the integration.

When doing written, rather than oral, sentence-completion work, you can use a notebook, typewriter, or computer.

Introductory Exercise

WEEK 1.

This first set, done for a week—Monday through Friday—is to help you become comfortable with the method. Later sets will take you deeper and deeper into self-awareness.

First thing in the morning, before proceeding to the day's business, sit down and write the following stem:

I am a person who—

Then, as rapidly as possible, without pausing for reflection, write as many endings as you can in two or three minutes—*never less than six, and ten is sufficient.* Do not worry whether your endings are "profound." Write anything, but write *something.* Never repeat the same ending twice on the same day. (In the course of a week, inevitably there will be some repetitions.)

Then go on to the next stem:

One of the things I wish people understood about me is—
   Then:
One of the things I wish I understood about people is—
   Then:
If I allowed myself to really see people—
   Then:
If I allowed people to really see me—
   Then:
I am becoming aware that—

The Basics

WEEK 2

If I bring five percent more awareness to my activities today—
If I bring five percent more awareness to my important relationships today—
If I bring five percent more awareness to my emotional reactions today—
If I bring five percent more awareness to my communications today—
I am becoming aware—

WEEK 3

If I bring five percent more awareness to my deepest fears today—
If I bring five percent more awareness to my deepest longings today—

If I bring five percent more awareness to the feelings other people
evoke in me—
If I can contemplate my feelings without self-judgment or
self-criticism—
I am becoming aware—

WEEK 4
If I imagine living more consciously—
The scary thing about living more consciously is—
If I bring five percent more awareness to my fear of living more
consciously—
If I bring five percent more awareness to the issues I tend to avoid—
Right now it seems obvious that—

WEEK 5
If I were more accepting of the different parts of me—
If I were more accepting of the strange thoughts and feelings I
sometimes have—
If I allowed myself to know all the different sides to me—
If I can accept even the parts of me that don't fit my self-image—
I am becoming aware—

Exploring the Influence of Parents

WEEK 6
Mother was always—
With Mother I felt—
Mother gave me a view of myself as—
One of the things I wanted from Mother and didn't get was—
Mother speaks through my voice when I tell myself—
I am becoming aware—

WEEK 7
Father was always—
With Father I felt—

Father gave me a view of myself as—
One of the things I wanted from Father and didn't get was—
Father speaks through my voice when I tell myself—
I am becoming aware—

WEEK 8
Mother gave me a view of life as—
Mother gave me a view of men as—
Mother gave me a view of women as—
Mother gave me a view of love as—
Mother gave me a view of sex as—

WEEK 9
Father gave me a view of life as—
Father gave me a view of men as—
Father gave me a view of women as—
Father gave me a view of love as—
Father gave me a view of sex as—
I am becoming aware—

WEEK 10
One of the unspoken messages I got from Mother was—
One of the unspoken messages I got from Father was—
If Mother thought I had a happy love relationship—
If Father thought I had a happy love relationship—
If Mother thought I had made a success of my life—
If Father thought I had made a success of my life—
I am becoming aware—

WEEK 11
If I reflect on Mother's influence in my life—
If I reflect on Father's influence in my life—
One of the things I'm still doing to win Mother's love is—
One of the things I'm still doing to win Father's love is—
If any of what I've written is true—

WEEK 12

One of the ways I'm like Mother is—
One of the ways I'm like Father is—
If it turns out I am more than my mother's child—
If it turns out I am more than my father's child—
If I am free to write my own life script—

Values

WEEK 13

One of the traits I look for in people is—
One of the rules I try to live by is—
I respect people most when they—
I don't respect people when they—
Sometimes I am drawn to people who—
Right now it seems to me that—

WEEK 14

One of the principles that guides me is—
One of the things I want out of life is—
One of the things I want from people is—
One of the things I want from work is—
One of the things I expect of myself is—
I am becoming aware—

WEEK 15

Life seems most fulfilling when—
Life seems most painful when—
When people speak of life as tragic—
When people speak of life as exciting—
I feel most alive when—
I am beginning to suspect—

Relationships

WEEK 16

If I bring five percent more awareness to my interactions with people—

If I bring five percent more awareness to my choice of companions—

One of the things I long for in relationships is—

One of the things that frustrate me in relationships is—

If I am honest with myself about my relationships—

WEEK 17

If were to treat listening as a creative act—

If I notice the effect I have on people—

If I notice how I respond to compliments—

If I notice how I respond to criticism—

If I pay attention to the quality of my communications—

WEEK 18

One of the things I want from people and often fail to get is—

One of the ways I can make it difficult for people to give me what I want is—

One of the ways I distance myself from people is—

With people, sometimes I'm afraid that—

One of the ways I can make my fears come true is—

WEEK 19

If I bring five percent more benevolence to my encounters with people—

If I were more willing to share my excitement—

If I were more willing to expose my vulnerability—

If I could face people with less self-protective armor—

I am becoming aware—

WEEK 20

If I look at my relationships realistically—
If I bring more awareness to my communications—
If I take more responsibility for being understood—
If I take more responsibility for understanding others—
I am becoming aware—

Resistance

WEEK 21

The scary thing about being more conscious is—
At the thought of operating more consciously—
If I operate unconsciously—
The good thing about raising my consciousness might be—
If I can face my fears without denial or disowning—

Conclusion

WEEK 22

If I am willing to see what I see and know what I know—
If I refuse to play "confused"—
If I am honest with myself about what I know—
If I keep reaching deeper within myself for answers—
If I fully accept that my mind is my most precious possession—
Right now I am very clear that—

Suggestion: When you have completed all 22 weeks of this program, take a week off and then do the program again, from the beginning, as if you had never done it before. You may be surprised by the changes in many of your responses, which will give you some indication of your progress on the road to living consciously . . . as well as the obstacles you may still need to work on overcoming.

▲ ▼ ▲

If you would like to share with me the results of your doing this program, I would be very happy to receive your feedback and observations. This will assist me in my own research, and perhaps I can be helpful to you.

I can be reached at:

P.O. Box 2609, Beverly Hills, California 90213

Phone: (310) 274–6361

Fax: (310) 271–6808

E-mail: N6666B@CS.com

Web: http://www.nathanielbranden.net

NOTES

Introduction

1. Price and wage controls are mentioned as a classic example. The great majority of economists recognize such controls to be counterproductive in the extreme; they tend to worsen the very conditions they aim to ameliorate. Other examples of counterproductive social legislation are given in *Taking Responsibility.*

Chapter 1   Living Consciously: First Principles

1. As Ayn Rand formulated the issue in *Atlas Shrugged:* "The law of causality is the law of identity applied to action. All actions are caused by entities. The nature of an action is caused and determined by the nature of the entities that act: a thing cannot act in contradiction to its nature." New York: Random House, 1957, 1037. An excellent discussion by a distinguished Aristotelian of how and why the law of identity necessitates the law of causality may be found in H. W. B. Joseph, *An Introduction to Logic,* second edition, chapter XIX. London: Oxford University Press, 1957.

2. For a superb discussion of this and related issues involving the development of mind, see Ayn Rand's *Introduction to Objectivist Epistemology,* second edition, edited by Harry Binswanger and Leonard Peikoff. New York: Meridian, 1990.

3. A second corollary of the law of identity is the law of the excluded middle, which states that a thing either is or is not A: an entity does or does not possess a particular attribute; a proposition is or is not true (at a given time and in a given respect).

4. For a fuller discussion of these issues, see *The Psychology of Self-Esteem,* New York: Bantam Books, 1969; and *The Six Pillars of Self-Esteem,* New York: Bantam Books, 1994.

5. I have attempted to make this discussion as nontechnical as possible, but readers familiar with philosophy will recognize that the epistemological and metaphysical perspective I am sketching here is Aristotelian/Objectivist. For a discussion of knowledge and consciousness, see *The Psychology of Self-Esteem,* ch. 3. As regards the revolt against reason and objectivity among twentieth-century philosophers, to which I briefly allude, a critique of their arguments is beyond the scope of this book. But see, for example, Brand Blanshard, *Reason and Analysis,* La Salle, Illinois: Open Court, 1991; and James F. Harris, *Against Relativism,* La Salle, Illinois: Open Court, 1993.

6. I discuss the volitional nature of thinking in some detail in *The Psychology*

of Self-Esteem. See also *Honoring the Self,* New York: Bantam Books, 1985; and *The Six Pillars of Self-Esteem.*

7. Mortimer J. Adler, *Intellect,* New York: Collier Books, Macmillan Publishing Company, 1990, 4–5.

Chapter 3   A Conscious Life—1: Knowing What We Are Doing While We Are Doing It

1. For a discussion of conscious, passionate love, see *The Psychology of Romantic Love,* New York: Bantam Books, 1981. For a discussion of conscious child-rearing, see *The Six Pillars of Self-Esteem,* New York: Bantam Books, 1994.

2. I have written a book entirely devoted to teaching people how to work with sentence completions at home—*The Art of Self-Discovery,* New York: Bantam Books, 1994.

Chapter 4   A Conscious Life—2: Bringing to Our Pursuits the Awareness They Require

1. See my discussion of psychological visibility in *The Psychology of Self-Esteem,* New York: Bantam Books, 1969; and *The Psychology of Romantic Love,* New York: Bantam Books, 1981.

2. I am indebted to Warren Farrell for this expression.

3. Her full statement, from which this is abstracted, is given in the chapter on self-responsibility and romantic love in *Taking Responsibility.* I observed in *The Psychology of Romantic Love* that no one can speak about this subject without, wittingly or unwittingly, making something of a personal confession.

4. In his essay "The Era of Conscious Action," in *Encyclopaedia Britannica Book of the Year, 1973.* For more on this issue, see my discussion in *The Six Pillars of Self-Esteem.*

Chapter 5   Self-Awareness: Examining Our Inner World

1. Of course these characterizations are oversimplified, but I believe they make the point.

2. See my description of this process in *Taking Responsibility.*

3. See my discussion in *Honoring the Self.*

Chapter 6   Consciousness and Self-Esteem

1. Sometimes I condense this definition to "self-esteem is the experience of being competent to cope with the challenges of life and of being worthy of happiness," but the longer formulation is more precise.

2. The justification for these assertions can be found in *The Six Pillars of Self-Esteem.*

3. Roy F. Baumeister, Joseph M. Boden, and Laura Smart, "Relation of Threatened Egotism to Violence and Agression: The Dark Side of High Self-Esteem," *Psychological Review* 103 (1996) 5–33.
4. Scott Mckeen, *Edmonton* (Alberta) *Journal,* March 18, 1996.

Chapter 7   Consciousness and Spirituality

1. Some later schools of Buddhism are theistic.
2. I understand, of course, that for a believer this observation may be very difficult to grasp, let alone accept. It is a weakness of our educational system that very few of us have been taught to recognize when terms and statements are meaningful and when they are not. We should not need to wait for philosophy classes in college to gain this information; it should be available at least at the high school level.
3. A concept I first introduced in a series of essays originally published in *The Objectivist Newsletter* in the 1960s, subsequently revised and integrated into the text of *The Psychology of Self-Esteem.*
4. For an admirably lucid presentation of the major "proofs" for God's existence and the philosophical rebuttal of those "proofs," see John Hospers, *Introduction to Philosophical Analysis,* third edition, chapter 7, Englewood Cliffs, New Jersey: Prentice Hall, 1988.
5. Jean Piaget, *The Essential Piaget,* New York: Basic Books, 1977.
6. L. Kohlberg, *Essays on Moral Development,* vol. 1, San Francisco: Harper, 1981. I strenuously disagree with Kohlberg's idea of what represents the highest level of development—he believes in an ethics of duty, unrelated to self-interest—whereas I advocate of an ethics of rational or enlightened self-interest, as I discuss in *Honoring the Self.*
7. David Hume. *Treatise of Human Nature,* London: Oxford University Press, 1978, 252.
8. W. T. Stace, *Mysticism and Philosophy,* London: Macmillan Press Ltd., 1980, 124.
9. For an elaboration of this point and an illuminating discussion of "self" as what she calls an "axiomatic concept," see Rand's *Introduction to Objectivist Epistemology,* expanded second edition, edited by Harry Binswanger and Leonard Peikoff. New York: Meridian, 1990, 251–256.
10. Ayn Rand, *Atlas Shrugged,* New York: Random House, 1957, 1015.
11. Stace, *Mysticism and Philosophy,* 321–22, 324.
12. Ken Wilber, *Up from Eden,* Garden City, New York: Anchor Press/Doubleday, 1981.
13. Ken Wilber, *Eye to Eye,* expanded edition. Boston and Shaftesbury: Shambhala, 1990, 3.
14. J. Levy, "Transpersonal and Jungian Psychology," *Journal of Humanistic Psychology,* vol. 23, no. 2, Spring 1983, 49.
15. Rand, *Atlas Shrugged,* 1031. While Rand and I have our disagreements, I admire her achievements enormously, and I consider her analysis of the

code of self-sacrifice in her hero's speech at the climax of the novel—from which I have briefly quoted—one of the most brilliant and devastating pieces of philosophical analysis I have ever read.

16. John Naisbitt, *Megatrends Asia,* New York: Simon & Schuster, 1996, 10.
17. Rand. *Atlas Shrugged,* 1052.

SELECTED BIBLIOGRAPHY

Adler, Mortimer J. *Intellect.* New York: Collier Books, 1980.

Baumeister, Roy F., Joseph Boden, and Laura Smart. "Relation of Threatened Egotism to Violence and Aggression: The Dark Side of High Self-Esteem." *Psychological Review* 103 (1996): 5–33.

Blanshard, Brand. *Reason and Analysis.* La Salle, Ill.: Open Court, 1991.

Branden, Nathaniel. *The Art of Self-Discovery.* New York: Bantam Books, 1993.

————. *Honoring the Self: Self-Esteem and Personal Transformation.* New York: Bantam Books, 1985.

————. *The Psychology of Romantic Love.* New York: Bantam Books, 1980.

————. *The Psychology of Self-Esteem.* New York: Bantam Books, 1969.

————. *The Six Pillars of Self-Esteem.* New York: Bantam Books, 1994.

————. *Taking Responsibility: Self-Reliance and the Accountable Life.* New York: Simon & Schuster, 1996.

Harris, James F. *Against Relativism.* La Salle, Ill.: Open Court, 1993.

Hitler, Adolph. *Mein Kampf.* Translated by Ralph Mannheim. Boston: Houghton Mifflin, 1943.

Hospers, John. *Introduction to Philosophical Analysis.* 3rd ed. New Jersey: Prentice Hall, 1988.

Hume, David. *Treatise of Human Nature.* 2nd ed. London: Oxford University Press, 1978.

Joseph, H. W. B. *An Introduction to Logic.* 2nd ed. London: Oxford University Press, 1957.

Kohlberg, L. *Essays on Moral Development.* vol. 1. San Francisco: Harper, 1981.

Levy, J. "Transpersonal and Jungian Psychology." *Journal of Humanistic Psychology* 23, no. 2 (Spring 1983).

Naisbitt, John. *Megatrends Asia.* New York: Simon & Schuster, 1996.

Piaget, Jean. *The Essential Piaget.* New York: Basic Books, 1977.

Rand, Ayn. *Atlas Shrugged.* New York: Random House, 1957.

————. *Introduction to Objectivist Epistemology.* 2nd ed. Edited by Harry Binswanger and Leonard Peikoff. New York: Meridian, 1990.

Stace, W. T. *Mysticism and Philosophy.* London: Macmillan, 1980.

Wilber, Ken. *Eye to Eye.* Expanded ed. Boston: Shambhala, 1990.

————. *Up from Eden.* New York: Anchor Press, 1981.

ACKNOWLEDGMENTS

Thanks first of all to my editor, Mary Ann Naples, for the clarity and insightfulness of her comments and requests, and for her overall enthusiasm for the project.

Next, I want to express my appreciation to the friends and colleagues who read different parts of the manuscript and gave helpful feedback: Dr. Warren Farrell, Dr. John Hospers, Darla Jasmine, Dr. David Kelley, Robert Reasoner, Dave Richo, Dr. Chris Sciabarra, Dr. Jim Sniechowski.

Special appreciation goes to my literary agent, Nat Sobel, not only for his friendship and unfailing support, but also for offering a number of excellent suggestions, including the idea of my writing an afterword.

And finally, my love and gratitude to my wife, Devers, for her enthusiastic feedback during the writing, her demands for more examples—and for creating an environment that contributes so much to making life at my computer a total joy.

INDEX

action dispositions, 167
actions, 50, 69, 94, 199
  in accordance with knowledge, 70–
    71, 158
  emotions and, 139, 150, 155–57,
    160–63
  feedback on, 87
  monitoring outcome of, 87–89
  regret concerning, 159
  relative to goals, 86–89
  responsibility for, 76–80
  sentence-completion exercise for,
    157–63
  unconscious, 52–53
Adler, Mortimer J., 41
aging, 227–28
Alice in Wonderland (Carroll), 196
alienation, state of, 29
  self-, 94, 130, 139, 154
Alzheimer's disease, 228
anger, 54, 55, 60, 139, 140–41, 160–61
anxiety, 29, 61–62, 68–69, 133
Apollo 13 crisis, 33–34
approval, desire for, 133, 176–77
Aquinas, Saint Thomas, 185
Aristotle, 23, 35, 71, 179, 185
"armor," body, 141
Arnold K. (case), 11–12
Asia, capitalism in, 222–26
atheism, 185, 186, 188–89, 205
Atlas Shrugged (Rand), 219, 225–26
Audrey W. (case), 129
avoidance, 25, 53–64, 175–76
  fatigue in, 53
  fear in, 53, 54–55, 56–60, 69, 89–
    91
  irrational indulgence of wishes as,
    53, 61–62
  irrelevant issues in, 55
  laziness in, 53, 55–56

managing impulses toward, 89–
    92
  mental passivity as, 53–54
  motives for, 53, 55–64
  pain in, 53, 54–55, 60–61
  self-deceiving subjectivism of, 68–
    69
  sentence-completion exercise for,
    91–92
  strategies of, 49–50, 53–55
  submergence in emotions as, 54–55
  of thinking, 48, 49
  see also evasion
awareness, 69–70, 75–76, 192, 228–
    229
  denial vs., 29–30
  of factors affecting self-esteem,
    175–77
  inner and outer, 28–33
  joy of, 71–76
  levels of, 44–53, 96–98, 103–4,
    109–10, 159–60
  see also self-awareness

Baumeister, Roy F., 173–75
"be here now," 67–68
being in the present, 52, 65, 66–69
beliefs, 28, 40, 58, 84, 122, 124–28,
    140, 191
  about emotions, 142, 156–57
  evidence needed for, 190
  internalized insults as, 77
  political, 124–25, 126–27, 217
  about self-esteem, 176–77
  unconsciousness of, 95–96, 124–26
  about workplace, 125
  see also God, belief in; religion;
    values
Boden, Joseph M., 173–75